THE MANBOOK

A Point-by-Point Guide to
Sucking It Up and Getting
the Job Done

NICK FREITAS

BROADSIDE BOOKS

Without limiting the exclusive rights of any author, contributor or the publisher of this publication, any unauthorized use of this publication to train generative artificial intelligence (AI) technologies is expressly prohibited. HarperCollins also exercise their rights under Article 4(3) of the Digital Single Market Directive 2019/790 and expressly reserve this publication from the text and data mining exception.

THE MANBOOK. Copyright © 2026 by Nick Freitas. All rights reserved. No part of this book may be used or reproduced in any manner whatsoever without written permission except in the case of brief quotations embodied in critical articles and reviews. For information, address HarperCollins Publishers, 195 Broadway, New York, NY 10007. In Europe, HarperCollins Publishers, Macken House, 39/40 Mayor Street Upper, Dublin 1, D01 C9W8, Ireland.

HarperCollins books may be purchased for educational, business, or sales promotional use. For information, please email the Special Markets Department at SPsales@harpercollins.com.

Broadside Books™ and the Broadside logo are trademarks of HarperCollins Publishers.

hc.com

FIRST EDITION

Designed by Michele Cameron

Library of Congress Cataloging-in-Publication Data has been applied for.

ISBN 978-0-06-343408-0

Printed in the United States of America

26 27 28 29 30 LBC 5 4 3 2 1

To Jesus Christ for redeeming me
To my beautiful wife, Tina, who always inspires me to be a better man
To my children, Lilly, Luke, and Ally, for becoming the kind of man and women parents dream of raising
To my mom for her courage, dedication, and servant's heart
To my dad, who worked to keep evil at bay so the innocent could sleep peaceably in their beds
To those I served with for always having my back when it counted
To Nate and Susie for being the kind of friends who would not only help hide a body but get rid of the witnesses
And to John Lovell, who I know looks up to me as a hero and the very personification of what it is to be a man. . . . Keep working, buddy, you'll get there one day
I couldn't have done it without you

CONTENTS

INTRODUCTION / What It Means to "Be a Man" / ix

LESSON 1 / How to Argue with Your Wife / 1

LESSON 2 / How to Prepare a Steak / 6

LESSON 3 / How to Kick in a Door / 10

LESSON 4 / How to Help Your Son Be Better Than You / 12

LESSON 5 / How to Flirt with Your Wife in Front of the Whole Family / 16

LESSON 6 / How to Give a Speech / 19

LESSON 7 / How to Build a Legacy / 24

LESSON 8 / How to Pick a Gun for Home Defense / 28

LESSON 9 / How to Stay in Shape for Your Wife / 33

LESSON 10 / How to Run for Public Office / 36

LESSON 11 / How to Drink Wine / 40

LESSON 12 / How to Drink Whiskey / 44

LESSON 13 / How to Have Great Sex / 46

LESSON 14 / How to Win a Fight / 51

LESSON 15 / How to Pick the "Right Woman" / 54

LESSON 16 / How to Pit a Car / 59

LESSON 17 / How to Never Have to Sleep on the Couch / 63

LESSON 18 / How to Teach Your Kids to Shoot / 66

LESSON 19 / How to Hot-wire a Car / 70

LESSON 20 / How to Talk About Your Wife / 73

LESSON 21 / How to Get Alpha Males to Work Together / 76

LESSON 22 / How to Parent as a Team / 81

LESSON 23 / How to Grow into a Man of God / 84

LESSON 24 / How to Be Dangerous FOR Your Family / 91

LESSON 25 / How to Cook for Others / 95

LESSON 26 / How to Make Your Daughter Feel Loved / 100

LESSON 27 / How to Win an Argument / 105

LESSON 28 / How to Learn from Your Parents / 113

LESSON 29 / How to Value Masculinity / 116

LESSON 30 / How to Conduct Basic First Aid / 120

LESSON 31 / How to Be the Head of Your Household / 125

LESSON 32 / How to Improve Your Appearance / 129

LESSON 33 / How to Lead in Your Marriage / 134

LESSON 34 / How to Craft a Logical Argument / 137

LESSON 35: / How to Craft an Effective Argument / 144

LESSON 36 / How to Admit You're Wrong to Your Kids / 147

LESSON 37 / How to Defend Your Faith / 151

LESSON 38 / How to Intimidate Your Daughter's Date / 160

LESSON 39 / How to Set Up a Date / 162

LESSON 40 / How to Date Your Wife / 169

LESSON 41 / How to Defend the Second Amendment / 175

LESSON 42 / How to Prepare Your Kids for Their First Job / 182

LESSON 43 / How to Argue in Front of Your Kids / 187

LESSON 44 / How to Protect Your Kids from Woke Nonsense / 190

LESSON 45 / How to Show Your Wife Gratitude / 197

LESSON 46 / How to Know What You Are Willing to Die For / 199

LESSON 47 / How to Know When It's REALLY OKAY to Cry / 205

LESSON 48 / How to Argue for Pro-Life / 208

LESSON 49 / How to Maintain Capabilities Instead of Just Stories / 212

LESSON 50 / How to Teach Your Kids About "Sharing" / 216

LESSON 51 / How to Argue for Free Market Capitalism / 219

LESSON 52 / How to Teach Your Kids to Date / 226

LESSON 53 / How to Teach Your Kids to Love America / 231

CLOSING ARGUMENTS / 235

INTRODUCTION

WHAT IT MEANS TO "BE A MAN"

Every guy has had the phrase "be a man" directed at him at some point in his life. And even though there are a lot of different ideas about what a man is, from scientific, anthropological, biological, sociological, and cultural perspectives, ask any guy what the phrase "be a man" means, and he will probably give you some version of this: **"Suck it up and get the job done."**

And he would be right. Being a man, at its most fundamental level, means prioritizing keeping your word, accomplishing the mission, "getting it done," regardless of discomfort, pain, or fear. That's what it means to be a man.

At least it used to.

We're currently living in an environment where we are finding out what happens when "being a man" gets redefined by a group of people who don't have a great deal of respect for men in general and traditional masculinity specifically. And it turns out, no one is happy with the results, including some of the most vociferous feminists behind the recent changes.

Now let's be fair. It would be easy to sit here and blame fourth-wave feminists, the "woke," this "messed-up generation," or any other group in order to absolve ourselves of responsibility, but to do that would be to both ignore the part men have played in allowing for this tragic redefinition and let us get distracted from the role we need to be playing within society if it is to be saved.

Righting the ship is going to be irritating, painful, and potentially even dangerous. But if we want masculinity to once again be appreciated for the vital role it plays in civilization, then it's our job to not only properly define it, not only advocate for it, but effectively demonstrate it at a time when it is least appreciated, but perhaps the most needed.

This book is a collection of lessons learned through life experiences—growing up, marriage, parenting, military service, politics, and business. It's a guide to navigating life's challenges through five key categories: spiritual, intellectual, emotional, physical, and professional.

> **The Spiritual:** Questions about God and morality are unavoidable. If God exists, He provides the foundation for truth and morality. Without Him, these concepts lack ultimate authority, reducing them to preferences. My worldview is rooted in Christianity, which shapes how I approach every aspect of life. This foundation is critical because it influences how we process information and approach the other categories.
>
> **The Intellectual:** This is about logic, reason, and the pursuit of wisdom—applying knowledge to practical and moral challenges. Intellectual growth requires curiosity, critical thinking, and a commitment to learning. It's not about mastering everything but developing the ability to think critically and lead confidently.
>
> **The Emotional:** Emotional maturity involves understanding and managing emotions while sympathizing with others. It's

essential for self-control and effective interaction. Emotional intelligence complements intellectual ability, ensuring that knowledge is communicated with care and connection.

The Physical: Physical health supports your ability to provide, protect, and lead. Good habits—exercise, healthy eating, and discipline—build strength and resilience. Genetics may set limits, but effort and consistency shape your physical presence.

The Professional: Professional skills enable you to provide value in the marketplace. Focus on developing capabilities, not just credentials. Success comes from understanding supply and demand, acquiring marketable skills, and balancing income with purpose and family priorities.

These five pillars shape every aspect of life.

This book is dedicated not only to every man who wants to be strong and capable but also to those who wish to be good men.

I don't claim to be the ultimate standard of such a man, but I do believe that a standard exists. And striving for it over the last forty-six years, through a broken home, marriage, fatherhood, war, politics, and everything in between, has taught me some lessons.

Here they are.

THE MANBOOK

LESSON 1

HOW TO ARGUE WITH YOUR WIFE

1. Remember you are talking to the woman you love.

2. Words and tone matter.

3. So do facts.

4. The goal is not to "defeat your wife." It's to come to the same conclusion.

"Don't argue with your wife, just apologize and say, 'Yes, dear.'" This is bad advice that unhappy old husbands give to new, naive ones.

Look, if you think placating your wife by treating her like someone who isn't worth your time is going to lead to a happy marriage, just ask the same guy giving you that advice if he is happy in his.

I argue with my wife when I think she is wrong, and guess what? She appreciates it. That's right! It turns out that when done properly, arguing with your wife is a form of problem-solving where both of you get on the same page about an issue or course of action, which is exactly where you want to be because you guys are in this together.

"But Nick, my girlfriend gets all hurt and emotional and holds a grudge if I argue with her."

Cool . . . then break up with her. Certainly don't marry her until you have figured out how to have disagreements that can turn into problem-solving sessions.

If you're already married or thinking of becoming so, here are some things I have learned.

I remember early on in my marriage, my beautiful young wife looked at me with a gaze that was clearly meant for someone she wanted to kill and, in a tone that indicated she was in fact capable of murder, said, "You need to speak to me like I am the woman you love."

In the heat of an argument between two very passionate people, neither of whom likes being wrong, it would have been very easy to dismiss this as a tactic. A debate trick to buy time by distracting from the context of the argument to address tone. But the seriousness in her voice caused me to pause and consider her point. Namely, that she was . . . in fact . . . right: She was and is the woman I love. Yes, we were having an argument, and yes, I was very sure I was right, but what was the point of the argument?

Did I just want to "win," or did I want to convince her of something? Was there some imaginary person keeping score, or was the purpose of the argument to successfully adjudicate a disagreement in such a way that both of us felt more in control of the situation, and the best way forward was not for "one of us" but for both of us?

If it were just to win, then screw my tone. If I'm right, then I'm right. Facts are facts, and according to Ben Shapiro, and reality, they don't care about your feelings . . . or mine, for that matter. But I did care. And facts weren't the only thing involved in this conversation, so winning did not mean defeating my wife. It meant both of us arriving at the truth so we could move forward together.

Tone matters. That's a fact.

Now, let me point out something very important here. I didn't stop arguing after this exchange. Rather, I changed my perspective on the purpose of the argument and my goals associated with it. Because the moment I said "I do," I committed myself to her for life, and she did the same for me. That means we are going to have disagreements. And you won't typically see me back down from a disagreement if I believe I am correct. Not because I'm argumentative (okay, I kind of am), but because I am committed to her and our marriage.

I want her to argue with me if she thinks I'm wrong. I want her to argue with me as the man she loves and respects, and she wants me to do the same for her.

Any guy who tells you "Don't bother arguing" is a guy who has either done a horrible job in choosing his bride or is too lazy to do what needs to be done to facilitate difficult but necessary conversations in his marriage.

My wife and I argue. Sometimes she is right, sometimes I'm right. Both of us are willing to admit when the other is right and, even more important, when we are wrong. But both of us work to remember that "winning the argument" means both of us have a better understanding of the problem, each other's perspective, and our ultimate end state, which is always our marriage is stronger for the exchange.

There are going to be times when you don't feel loving. There are going to be times when she does not remember to speak to you with respect. I am not telling you to put up with disrespect. I am saying that the situation will not improve if you respond with condescension or demeaning comments. Never go after her vulnerabilities. Whatever is going on, there is the rest of your marriage after this argument, so remember that. I argue hard with my wife at times, but I try not to do or say anything that would make her doubt my love or commitment to her. It's really that simple.

Before you get married: Discuss things of actual importance with someone you're dating. In fact, lead with it. I'm not saying you have to ask a woman on the first date how many kids she wants to have, but if you're dating with the intention of marriage, then understanding how she thinks about topics and the kind of reasoning and tactics she uses in disagreements is pretty important. After you're married, it's about working with what you have, for both of you. So, practice discussing issues of disagreement in such a way that you both feel that the other one has your back. Sometimes it doesn't hurt to preface it with "Hey, I know we might disagree on this. I want to see if we can figure it out, but either way it's me and you, babe. I don't want to defeat you; I want our marriage to win." If she feels confident that you are there for her, no matter what, and that you are also willing to admit when you are wrong, it will provide her with the security she needs to do the same.

> **Speak to each other like you love one another.** Don't say things in the heat of the moment that will cause your wife to question your love or respect for one another. Men, your wife needs to feel supported, so make sure that the words you use reinforce that you are on her side. I NEVER call my wife names or hit her insecurities to score cheap points. Ladies, even when my wife is pretty angry with me, or the debate is heated, she still speaks to me with respect.

> **Logic matters.** Feelings don't trump facts, logic, or overwhelming evidence. But if the feeling won't go away, parse it. Men, don't discount a woman's discernment. I can't tell you how many times my wife has had a "feeling" about something that she couldn't quite explain that turned out to be right. Ladies, one of the things I truly appreciate about my wife is that she will stay on topic, and if I have made a good point, she acknowledges it, rather than changing the subject or moving on. I try to do the same for her.

The goal is agreement, not victory. You're not trying to "defeat" one another in an argument; you're trying to get to the bottom of an issue so that you can tackle it together. You will be shocked by how that mindset can change the way you look at the argument.

LESSON 2

HOW TO PREPARE A STEAK

Contrary to popular opinion, there are only two acceptable temperature ranges for steak. Rare and medium rare. Everything after that is either a mistake, which turns steak into sandwich meat, or a crime against humanity.

However, to be transparent, there are technically five temperature ranges for cooking meat. I am going to use Fahrenheit because that's what we use in America, and since we have the best nukes, we win.

Rare: 120–125° F (cool red center)

Medium Rare: 130–135° F (warm red center)

Medium: 140–145° F (warm pink center)

Medium Well: 150–155° F (slightly pink center)

Well Done (which is anything but): 160° F (no pink center)

This is the portion of the chat where one side will come in and say, "What about threatened with a lit match and blue?" and the other will say, "This is garbage, you just don't know how to properly cook a well-done steak."

To those of you who like to eat the steak while it's still grazing in the pasture, you do you. And to those of you who think I don't know how to burn a steak: I do. I just don't think it should be done.

Growing up, I would have told you that the best steak was a rib eye, medium rare. As I got into my twenties, I would have said it was a New York strip, medium rare. In my thirties, prime rib, medium rare. And while I still love all those options, I have to say that now, in my forties, my favorite cuts are actually tri-tip or sirloin picanha. Allow me to explain.

Growing up, I had always loved tri-tip, which was kind of a "West Coast thing." I remember being stationed on the East Coast, and most restaurants and stores hadn't even heard of tri-tip, let alone carried it. That's probably because this bottom portion of the sirloin, in a triangular shape, is usually processed as part of something else rather than reserved as its own cut. (It's sometimes just ground into ground sirloin in the East, but it may also be sold as a Newport roast.) Sirloins have some of the richest flavors of all the cuts, but are usually not as tender. This particular portion is both rich in flavor and fairly tender. You can cook it in a number of ways, but I think the best is roasting and then cutting it up into strips.

I was introduced to sirloin picanha for the first time at a Brazilian steak house. For those of you who don't know what that is, it's a magical place where the most savory and delicious of meats are brought to your table for as long as you want or until they close. It works like this.

You pay a flat rate and are escorted to your table past a very impressive salad bar, which I believe they use as a trick to try to fill you up. Or perhaps as an option for vegans who clearly have friends with better taste than they possess, but I digress. You sit at your table and are informed of a coaster, which has a red and a green side. When you desire your table to be flooded with gauchos carrying spits of meat to provide you with options, you turn it green. And when you desire sadness, you turn it red.

Now you may be thinking, with options like "bacon-wrapped filet," who would go for the sirloin picanha? But I'm telling you, there is a reason why that is their signature cut. "But Nick, if it is so good, it must be an incredibly expensive cut," you proclaim with understandable scrutiny. NO! It isn't! You can find it for approximately eight dollars a pound as I write this in the fall of 2024. It's all about how you prepare and cook it. (It may be sold as top cap sirloin where you shop.)

Now, I delve into the Freitas method for preparing and cooking these two cuts of beef.

We are not a wet marinade family. Nothing against the people who are, and I have had some excellent ones, but we prefer the dry rubs. Montreal seasoning is our all-time favorite and go-to. We will pack that cut with Montreal and then move it to the grill, which in our case is a Big Green Egg. Now, if you don't know what that is, you will want to look it up. After looking it up, you will most likely conclude that this is some sort of "grill cult" with its many rituals, recipes, and insatiable desire to evangelize. You might be a little right, but trust me, once you get past the initial sticker shock, it becomes the last grill you will ever own.

We heat up the lump charcoal (must be lump!) and then place the top cap sirloin or tri-tip on the Kamado Joe "JoeTisserie," which is a rotisserie add-on and well worth it. Cook that baby to temp. Always to temp! Cooking to time is just dangerous. And remember, if you are cooking rare or medium rare, you need to remove it about 5–10 degrees shy of where you want it to land. But once you have it there, take it off, let it sit for a little bit, and then cut it up into slices. Resting your meat is essential. You can thank me later.

The other cuts we regularly use are rib eyes, New York strips, and various sirloins from Good Ranchers, which are incredible. We both grill those and cook them in a cast-iron skillet. The benefit to the skillet is copious amounts of butter; you must use it both for taste and to ensure that the meat doesn't stick to the pan. No seed oils! Just lots of actual butter.

Again, take the meat out of the package, add Montreal seasoning (butter the pan if using a cast-iron skillet), and then cook to temp! Remove about 5–10 degrees shy of where you want it to land and then serve!

Now is the part where I come clean about something. In our house, my wife is the one doing this most of the time because she is incredible at it. I used to love going out to steak houses, but now I am almost always disappointed because the way she cooks a steak is the way I think it should be for my taste and preferences. Plus, she is on a carnivore diet.

In the end, you must find a cut, seasoning, and temperature that works best for you. I give people who like a medium-well or well-done steak a lot of grief because I honestly believe that they deserve it for their many crimes against the Bovinae subfamily, but ultimately, this is about taste, and as long as you're eating steak, you're still probably a much better person than a vegan.

If you are someone who thinks you don't really like steak, I'm going to suggest that you try one medium rare or rare prepared by someone who loves steak and knows how to cook it. I have run into too many people who thought they either didn't like steak or preferred it well done, only to find out they really love it when prepared properly and served at a lower temperature.

LESSON 3

HOW TO KICK IN A DOOR

Why would you ever need to kick in a door? Well, in the event you ever need to, believe me, you're going to want to know. I had to learn for the obvious reason that I spent over eleven years in infantry and Special Forces units in the military. Turns out, opening doors people didn't want you to open was part of the job description.

But let's clarify something before we go any further. Kicking in a door is not something you do just so you can look "badass." Knowing how to properly gain entry to a room you may need to is about being able to protect someone or something from danger, while avoiding injury . . . and looking totally badass in the process.

The first thing you want to do is establish that the door does actually need "kicking in" or some other form of blunt force trauma to gain entry.

Next, it pays to know that the door opens inward instead of outward. The best way to turn a supercool "Daddy's home," kick-in-the-door moment to you looking like an idiot is kicking a door in the opposite direction of which it naturally swings. In such cases, you either get abruptly stopped and potentially injure yourself, or if your placement is off, your leg ends up through the door, and now not only are you in a vulnerable position but you look stupid, and we can't have that!

Once you have established that (1) door requires kicking and (2) door opens in the direction I'm kicking it, you can move on to (3) kick the door in the right place, which is typically just under the doorknob, as close to the strike plate area as possible. The point is to apply force close to where the latching mechanism engages with the strike plate. Too far to the right and you hit the frame. Too far to the center of the door will either blunt your force if it's a solid-core door or, again, create a big hole your leg goes through if the door is hollow.

The mechanics of kicking it are pretty simple. You're going to take a step toward the door with your nondominant leg, planting your foot with enough space between you and the door so that when you kick, your foot should be vertical and your leg is partially (NOT fully) extended when your foot hits the door.

It does feel and look cool when you get it right.

Back to the original question of "when would you ever need to do this?" How about getting your kids out of a building fast because it's on fire? How about one of your kids screaming for help behind a locked door? The odds of these things happening may be low, but being a man means knowing how to do certain things in dangerous moments so that you can protect the people you love.

LESSON 4

HOW TO HELP YOUR SON BE BETTER THAN YOU

1. Your son needs to know that you love him.

2. You need to challenge him spiritually, intellectually, emotionally, physically, and professionally.

3. Build trust with him.

4. Set the example by being a man worthy of his respect.

"Your son is your replacement in the world."

I made this statement once in a video I did on YouTube, and some genius in the comments replied that this was "ridiculous." It's not like your son is going to marry your wife or become your kids' parent when you're gone.

Yeah... no kidding. Thanks for that, Chief. Also, you missed the point entirely.

Your son is not your literal replacement. But his upbringing is your responsibility, and he is a part of your legacy. He will fill a role, in fact, many of the roles in society that you once did. Husband, father, protector, provider, among many others that he may be called upon to play in the event that his family, community, or country requires it. The question you will need to ask yourself is: Did you prepare him for that?

My own son will have left for the military by the time this book is published. So, I find myself asking whether I did everything I could have to ensure that he was properly prepared. The answer to that is no. There is always something more you could have done, and I am sure I will continue to consider this question over the years. That's what fathers do.

But I am confident of several things that give me a great deal of peace. I am sure that his faith in Christ is his own. That he understands right from wrong. That he knows he has a duty to be responsible and brave. And I am sure that he has a good foundation on which to build his own life and family.

I am now moving into that phase of life with my son where he is becoming his own man. He will now face an ever-increasing set of challenges where my ability to intercede on his behalf is either limited or nonexistent. I knew this day would come, and so did he. As a result, we prepared for it. And now, I believe he is ready, but he will have to prove it.

So, how does a father set his son up for success?

Here are a few things I would recommend to fathers of sons.

Your son needs to know that you love him. That means saying it and demonstrating it through devoting time to his development and his interests. It also means including him in your interests and work.

You need to challenge your son. This starts earlier than you may think. Challenges should always be age-appropriate, but from the time he is old enough to walk, dads should be challenging their sons to be tough, to try again, to be responsible.

When he's little, it's usually telling him to get up when he falls down and not allowing him to cry in order to manipulate others. I don't care how many women say they want a man who's "not afraid to cry" because they sure as hell don't respect one who does it frequently. There are times when it is appropriate to cry, and I discuss that, but teaching your son early on that crying doesn't get you what you want is important.

When he gets older, the challenges should become more complex. Sometimes it's having him help you with a project and giving him encouragement. Other times, it's giving him his own space to work and figure things out. Even when they're little, you're building both capability and confidence. But be careful. Building confidence separate from capability breeds arrogance and entitlement. Boys need to understand that they can and should try things, hard things, that they may not be immediately good at. And it's good to encourage them, especially when they're little, to have sufficient confidence to not be immediately discouraged by defeat or mistakes. But they also have to be encouraged to learn from them.

As they get older, they will gravitate to the things they are interested in and good at. And that might not be what Dad is interested in or good at. So be ready to adapt and learn new things along with your son.

Your son being your replacement doesn't mean he is a carbon copy. It means he is fulfilling certain responsibilities that civilization requires from men and that God requires from all of us. When it comes to issues of character, responsibility, and truth, you direct. When it comes to interest, skills, and capabilities, you guide. God has a purpose for your son, and your job is to help him discover and prepare for it.

Build trust. You want your son to be able to discuss things with you. This means he has to trust that he can come to you with issues that matter and receive good advice.

Finally, and this is very important: You need to be worthy of teaching him.

Men, this is one of the scariest and most hopeful things you will read in this book. Think back on all the men in your life you know. How many of them are trying to either live up to their dads or be the farthest thing from them they can? Regardless of which one it is, how many of them want to prove something to their father?

That is how much power you have as a dad. You have it if you show up, and you have it if you don't. That means it's nonnegotiable. You don't get to walk away because even if you do, the responsibility is still there; it will just get picked up by someone else. And maybe, if you're lucky, the man who does pick it up will be a good one. But if he isn't, that's on you.

I don't think our society can take much more of the kind of men whose dads didn't show up. I'm not telling you that you have to be perfect. One of the greatest blessings God ever gave us was being perfect enough for all of us. But He did give us something to strive for.

The good news is your son desperately wants you to be a good man, a champion, his hero. And you will never be sorry for having done everything you could to prove him right.

LESSON 5

HOW TO FLIRT WITH YOUR WIFE IN FRONT OF THE WHOLE FAMILY

Telling a guy he should flirt with his wife is pretty standard, but why "in front of your kids"? Well, first of all, flirt with your wife all the time. At home, alone, in public, and yes, in front of your kids.

Now, obviously, it should be flirting that is appropriate for the location and context. I'm saying this for the people already gearing up to explain all the ways that flirting could be inappropriate at a funeral . . . yes Karen, thank you . . . but the point is not only is flirting with your wife good for your marriage, it's good for your family.

A while back, I did a Reel where I said I was going to address the very controversial issue of whether I supported spanking . . . as half of my audience watched in anticipation of whether they were going to continue to follow me, I declared that I was in favor of an appropriate spank now and again . . . primarily whenever my wife walked by. Most people got the joke. One guy in Portland got very upset with me, but I think he's just lonely. Anyway, the point is there is no shortage of advice telling you to flirt with your wife or your husband to show them they still have it. And I couldn't agree more.

The reason I encourage husbands and wives not to refrain from that sort of age-appropriate banter in front of your kids is that no matter how much they grimace or make vomiting sounds, kids like to know that Mom and Dad not only love each other but still think the other one "has it."

When husband and wife expand to include father and mother, the kids end up taking a lot of your time and attention. It can be easy to fall into roles and start behaving more as roommates or companions than as two people in love with one another. A married couple who still flirt with each other is a good sign that the fundamentals of that relationship are still strong. Mom and Dad being hot for one another actually provides kids with a lot of security, not to mention positive expectations for their own marriage one day.

I know this not only because it makes sense, but because my kids have told me. As they got older and even picked up on some of the innuendo a little better than we thought they would, there was always a little bit of embarrassment. However, they also picked up on the knowledge that Mom and Dad still love each other, and all is right with the world. The home is safe. The people who raised them not only love them but also love each other. It shouldn't be a surprise that kids who grow up in happy homes usually want to have homes of their own, and often at a younger age.

By the same token, kids who don't have this in their home wish they did. And it affects more than just how they feel about the security of their home. It affects how they seek out affection. When Mom and Dad behave as if they tolerate one another, chances are affection is lacking in more than just the marital relationship. There is a tension that comes over a home that causes people not only to want to escape it but to seek out the thing that is obviously lacking.

If affection, intimacy, and security can't be found at home, your kids will seek it in other places, in ways that they are probably not ready for, and with people who either struggle with the same thing or lack the maturity to make wise decisions.

It may sound weird, but flirting with your wife is a subtle way to demonstrate to your kids that the home is safe and that marriage is the proper place to seek out affection. One of my kids once told me a story about a friend of theirs who said they wished their parents flirted like hers. They just wanted to know that their parents loved each other. So yeah, your kids are going to contort or run out of the room or maybe even tell you you're inappropriate, but deep down, they know it means there is stability. And that one day, they will get to have that with the person they love.

For anyone who didn't get the first couple of caveats, I'm not talking about making out with your wife while your kids have their friends over or copping a feel at church. Although, to be perfectly honest, that doesn't mean I haven't tried the last one. Don't worry, it was very tasteful, and no one saw . . . I'm pretty sure.

So, whistle at your wife, tell her how hot she is (and encourage her to look her husband up and down a little longer than is appropriate in polite company), and know that a mom and a dad still hot for each other after all these years is ultimately what most people want one day. Don't be afraid to brag that you have it.

LESSON 6

HOW TO GIVE A SPEECH

1. Be authentic.

2. Be relevant to your audience.

3. Be brief.

This is an interesting chapter for me to write, and here is why. The last formal training I received on giving a speech was Speech and Debate in tenth grade in a high school with a graduating class of twenty-seven. I did get some informal training on how to deliver a presentation or an intelligence report while I was in the military, but all my experience has essentially been OJT (on-the-job training). In fact, when I was first considering running for office, I remember my wife saying, "I think you would be great, I'm just not sure you could give a 'political speech.'"

Having admitted all that, I should briefly provide some credentials for why you should read the rest of this chapter or care about my advice.

The first time I thought I might have a knack for giving a speech was when I spoke on Memorial Day at the Culpeper National Cemetery. The year before, the speech had been given by a distinguished local historian who spoke for somewhere around thirty minutes, if I remember correctly. I was asked to speak the next year, and I almost made it to six minutes. But the reception I received was overwhelmingly positive. I still have the beautifully framed picture of me and my family presented to me by the local American Legion, which has hung in my legislative office ever since.

In my first year in the General Assembly, I gave my first "viral speech." It was about a Green Beret named SFC Charles Martland who was being forced to retire because he had beaten a child rapist in Afghanistan. I believed, as did most of my colleagues, that he deserved a medal rather than a discharge, and we were able to play a small part in ensuring that he was allowed to continue to serve in the Army.

But it was in 2018, shortly after the Parkland shooting, that I gave a seven-minute speech defending the Second Amendment that first took me into the national spotlight. That speech got around one hundred million views on social media and got me a spot on Sean Hannity's show, as well as others. It was shared by Ben Shapiro, Ted Nugent, and many others.

What made that particular speech special is that at the time, many people felt as if very few politicians were willing not only to give an impassioned defense of our rights but to actually take the other side of the aisle to task on both the manner in which they discussed the issue and the real conditions that led to violence. The comments were very clear: The speech had made them feel heard and defended, in a difficult time, but more than that, it made them feel as if someone had finally stuck up for them.

So why did it work?

Well, I don't use notes. I spoke from the heart. Say what you want about the overall argument I used, but there was little doubt in anyone's mind that I had studied the issue, and more than that, I genuinely cared about it.

And it hit home, because for weeks, this is what the nation had been talking about. One side of the debate had already decided what the solution was, and if you disagreed, you weren't just wrong, you were evil, and people were tired of hearing that. They didn't want someone to bashfully suggest that there was another perspective. They wanted someone to boldly defend their position AND then go on offense. For the audience that loved that speech, it couldn't have been more relevant.

And finally, it was not a forty-five-minute lecture or even an eighteen-minute TED talk, it was a seven-minute speech, with several parts that you could clip into twenty-to-sixty-second sound bites, which made it easy to digest and easy to share.

When I am invited to speak to a group, I typically follow these steps.

1. I ask the organizers what they would like me to address. This is both to be respectful to the people having me come and speak and to elicit from the people who know the audience better than I do what they expect to hear. This ensures that your remarks are relevant.

2. I then think about the opening of the speech. The opening is critical. Short attention span is a natural response to the fact that we literally have thousands of messages thrown at us daily, and with so many things vying for our attention, we look for the things that truly matter to us. The opening is where you generate both interest and connection to your audience. I usually like to start with a story.

3. Next, I think about the main points I want to make and how I want to make them. This usually includes other stories. Some funny, some thoughtful, some potentially sad. It depends on what emotion is appropriate for the subject matter.

4. Then I think a lot about how to stick the landing. This is where a lot of speeches go wrong, because people can't find where they want to land, ramble on for too long, and eventually crash. It's important because no one is going to remember everything you say. They're not going to remember most of what you said. But sticking that landing will make them feel satisfied with your speech. It is like delivering on a promise. Maybe they agreed, maybe they had issues with some of it, maybe they loved all of it, but sticking the landing sets a tone for how it will be remembered.

5. Throughout this entire process, I am thinking about the tone or emotions in each part. Because people may forget the specific words you used, but they won't forget how you made them feel. If I have fifteen minutes or more to speak, I usually try to make the audience laugh, think, cry, and act. The laughing creates connection, the thinking engages the brain, the crying engages the sense of longing and compassion, and the act speaks to their desire to fight for something greater than themselves and to be worthy of a noble cause.

6. How do I know each of those things will land? I think about it and say it to myself, and then ask myself, is what I'm saying right now making me feel those emotions I am trying to invoke? If the answer is yes, then I'm onto something. If the answer is no, then I'm trying to force something

I don't even feel, so how can I expect the audience to?
More work is needed because authenticity is critical.

Everyone has different comfort levels and styles. My good friend Rob Bell, who was a delegate for twenty years in the General Assembly, once said that some speakers are funny, some are passionate, and his style was always analytical and sincere. But the only time I ever cried on the House floor was when he gave his retirement speech. Not because he was trying for it, but because every minute of his speech was authentic and from the heart.

There is a lot to be said for simply speaking from the heart . . . unless you're an idiot. Then you just come off as a very sincere moron.

LESSON 7

HOW TO BUILD A LEGACY

1. Teach your kids about the family's past and help them feel connected to it.

2. Provide visualizations through pictures, shadow boxes, keepsakes, and so on.

3. Include their accomplishments as part of the history of the family.

4. Live up to the example the best of them set.

I spent a great deal of time with my paternal grandfather. We would spend time in his den, which smelled of pipe tobacco and was decorated with guns, swords, campaign ribbons, reloading equipment, and pictures. It felt like a family museum. I can still remember three small shadow boxes he had on the wall. The first was of my great-grandfather, whom I had never met. It featured his picture in uniform and various badges he had worn as a law enforcement officer in California.

The next was my grandfather as a fire captain and the various badges he had worn throughout a lifetime of service in the fire department.

Then there was my father with his badges from the LAPD, police officer and detective, as well as the ribbons he had earned in service in some of the most dangerous areas of Los Angeles as a patrolman and a homicide detective.

I can remember, quite vividly, what it was like to be a small boy looking up at the pictures of the men who had come before me, the accomplishments they had, the stories they shared of dangers they faced, friends lost, and the antics that took place between friends with a special bond found in occupations where coming home after work is not a foregone conclusion.

Ten dollars. That's what each of those shadow boxes costs to make. A simple frame, a picture, a little bit of felt, and a few badges and ribbons. But only a few times in my life have I felt the same sense of accomplishment and belonging as when I came home on leave from the military to find that my shadow box was now on the wall. I had earned my place in the pantheon of Freitas Men.

Don't ever underestimate the power of sharing with your son the stories of where he came from. Let him listen in as you and your father discuss the good times, the bad times, the successes, and the failures that forged you into what you are.

Your story will be told one way or another. Maybe by friends or family, maybe the press or historians, but it will be told. Ensure that you have your say in your own story. It may be the simple shadow box, the photos, or the occasional stories broken out every so often that let your children and grandchildren know that they are a part of something bigger. Ensure that your children know where they come from and instill in them a desire to leave that legacy better than when they found it, so that one day their kids can do the same.

"But Nick . . . I don't have a legacy." I had someone respond to me with this.

I didn't know who he was or anything about his background. It was just a comment, written out somewhat dismissively in response to something I had said. But it lingered.

There were hundreds of other comments giving me the e-version of fist bumps and telling me how encouraging and profound my statement was. And yet this guy's comment hung there on my phone and in my mind, because it felt like I had just bragged about how great my steak dinner was in front of a starving orphan.

It would have been so much easier to ignore if he had been a punk about it. Flippantly telling me I didn't know what I was talking about or suggesting I was "privileged," but there was none of that. Just a simple statement that reminded me that there are a lot of men out there whose only experience with legacy is listening to other men talk about it.

The thing is, he did have a legacy. It was just starting with him.

There is no question that any man living today should be able to look back on the men in his line with a sense of pride and belonging. But some don't. Which means it starts with them.

And while it is not ideal, and nothing about this fact is easy or to be spoken of flippantly, it's still the truth. And an incredible one if you really think about it. Imagine a long line of failure, decades, if not centuries long, that ends abruptly and completely because you ended it. Because you refused to repeat the failures of the men who failed you. That is the kind of man from whom legacies are built, preserved, and passed on.

You should have had a father who provided you with a legacy. Instead, you were provided with the opportunity to be the first. The divergence in the history of your family, to which your future son, grandson, and great-grandson will look back and say, "That's when it began."

That is an incredible thing to consider.

Everyone has something they have to overcome. It's tougher for some than for others, but a victim mentality will never get you to where you want to be. There is no shame in having been denied things you were owed as a child, but neither does it represent an excuse to perpetuate it onto future generations. There is a reason we admire people who overcome challenges, break cycles, and improve the future for themselves and their families. So, choose to be that guy. Surround yourself with people whose character you admire and build for your children a legacy they will be proud to carry on.

LESSON 8

HOW TO PICK A GUN FOR HOME DEFENSE

What sort of gun should I have for home defense? I get asked this a lot, and it is a great question, because while there are a lot of reasons to own firearms, from hunting to target practice to defending against all enemies foreign and domestic, home defense is probably the most common, and certainly one of the most important.

Here are three things to consider right away.

1. **Who is going to be using it?** Is it you, you and your wife, or maybe an older child? Whatever firearm or arms are going to potentially be used for this purpose, everyone who might have to use them needs to be able to handle and understand how to use the chosen firearm.

2. **Where do you live?** Some places have more laws or regulations concerning firearms, and this will also affect what you can get and how it must be stored.

3. **What storage is required?** A weapon stored unloaded in a safe is not a home defense weapon. Ideally, a home defense weapon will be somewhere that is easily accessible and ready for use. If you do live in a commie state that demands ridiculous storage requirements, a push button combination or fingerprint safe might be the best option.

There are different opinions on whether you should get a shotgun or a pistol, and I will tell you that there can be good arguments for both. So, let's go through some pros and cons.

SHOTGUNS

PROS

1. Shotguns are fairly easy to use and aim.

2. The variety of ammunition available gives you a lot of options, including options that are less lethal, make it harder to miss, and are less likely to go through multiple walls, which is a major consideration if you have other people in the house or close neighbors.

3. They are also a good option if you have other uses for them such as hunting or managing larger vermin or small predators.

CONS

1. The size of shotguns, especially in places with stricter barrel or magazine capacities, can be cumbersome when moving in a home and difficult to point in a place with multiple corners.

2. Depending on the gauge, especially if it has a short barrel, a shotgun can have a greater kick.

3. In many places, a shotgun is not permitted to have an internal magazine that carries more than two rounds, which means you can have at most three rounds loaded at any time if you maintain one in the chamber.

Overall, a shotgun is just good to have, as it is a firearm with diverse capabilities, of which home defense is one. However, it is not my preferred firearm for home defense.

For pistols, we would need to consider semiautomatics versus revolvers, single action, and double action.

Semiautomatics are pistols that fire a round every time the trigger is pulled. The pistol uses the energy released from the firing of a round to move the slide to the rear, eject the spent cartridge, load another round into the chamber, and recock the weapon. They require an external magazine that can hold a number of rounds based on the size and caliber of both the pistol and the magazine, usually between eight and fifteen. The vast majority of pistols you see carried by police and the military are semiautomatic. The most obvious pro of the semiautomatic is greater round capacity and arguably a greater rate of fire. And the external magazine allows for fast reloading. The con is that they are technically less dependable than a revolver due to more moving parts.

A revolver is a pistol that features a cylinder, usually capable of holding between five and six rounds, which rotates as the trigger mechanism is pulled to allow for a new round to be available for each shot. A single-action revolver requires you to pull the hammer back manually, which engages the cylinder to rotate, and then the trigger is pulled. A double-action revolver requires that you pull only the trigger in order to both rotate the cylinder and recock the hammer. Most of your modern revolvers are double action. Most single-action revolvers are older models, usually associated with the Wild West, for a pop culture reference. (Picture the cowboy hero firing with one hand while repeatedly hitting the hammer back with the palm of his other hand.) The pros of a revolver are durability, reliability, ease of loading (in some respects), and suitability for novices, and they look cool. The cons are fewer rounds, slower rate of fire, and fewer safety features when it comes to smaller children getting a hold of them. (I'll explain in a minute.)

With all that in mind, my preference for a home defense weapon is a semiautomatic pistol with some form of hollow point rounds.

1. **More Rounds:** Look, unless you are very well trained, there is a good chance you might not get a hit on the first round. Not to mention that while you probably won't find yourself having to reload in a home defense situation, the option is nice, and changing out a magazine is a lot faster in most cases than reloading a revolver, even if you have a speed loader.

2. **Ergonomics:** I find the ergonomics or comfort of firing a semiautomatic to be better than a revolver. This can certainly be debated based on preference, but I believe the mechanics of a semiautomatic are better for multiple shots on target than a revolver.

3. **Safety Features:** While you can get safety features with both semiautomatics and revolvers, I think the features for a semiautomatic are superior. For example, I use the Springfield XD. The XD has a grip and trigger safety, which is neither cumbersome nor something you forget to disengage before firing. It also features a small indicator in the form of a lever on the top of the slide, letting you know that there is a round in the chamber, as well as a portion of the firing pin that slightly protrudes out of the back of the slide when the weapon is cocked.

If you are buying a weapon to protect your family, then you already have the right top priority: safety. Let's imagine the following scenario. Your wife is home alone while you are traveling. You have a three-year-old capable of walking, opening doors, and getting into mischief. Understanding that an unloaded gun is basically a blunt instrument and that in the panic and uncertainty of a home invasion, your wife might not feel confident in quickly loading an empty gun, she keeps her semi-automatic pistol on the nightstand next to her bed with the magazine loaded, but without a round in the chamber. She does this so that if for some reason the toddler got a hold of the firearm, there would be no way the child could rack the slide and load a round. By the same token, your wife has been trained in how to effectively pull the slide back. After doing so, she can feel the indicator on the top of and rear of the slide and be confident that her pistol is now loaded and cocked. She is now ready to defend herself and your child if needed very quickly.

Now please understand. I am not advocating that you buy a particular brand of semiautomatic. I'm merely providing insight into what has informed my decisions for my household. When I took my daughter to get her first gun, she chose a different brand based on her comfort level holding it and the sight configuration.

Ultimately, choose a home defense weapon based on the various criteria I have mentioned and then ensure that everyone knows how to properly load, unload, store, and utilize the firearm.

As a side note, we taught all our children (one boy, two girls) about firearms at a very young age, with them first shooting a pistol around the age of five. Hiding guns from your children is seldom the best way to teach them about responsible gun ownership. They should be respectful of what a firearm can do, not afraid of them. And while every child is different, we found that providing supervised access instilled in our children the proper respect for safety as well as understanding the proper use. This not only helped them better understand how to effectively own and use a firearm but protected them intellectually from emotionally charged rhetoric and bad arguments against private firearm ownership.

LESSON

HOW TO STAY IN SHAPE FOR YOUR WIFE

1. Men need to provide, and that is easier if you are in shape.

2. Men need to protect, and if you get in a fight, she should know you can actually go more than one round.

3. You're the only one she gets to sleep with, so try and make sure she is excited about seeing you naked . . . plus if you're in shape, you are more likely to be able to go more than one round.

Assuming you married a good and faithful woman, you're the last guy she ever gets to sleep with. Think about that for a second. I know that men are typically the ones more obsessed with physical beauty, but women have eyes too. And guys, I'm going to let you in on something . . . the attractive "dad bod" is not really a thing.

I get it. I still remember leaving the Army in my early thirties and teasing my wife that she should take a good look, because without the United States Army forcing me to run ten to twenty miles a week, I was never going to run again, unless I was being chased by the cops, and even then, it better be over serious charges for me to put in real effort.

For quite some time, I lived up to that promise. I was still active enough to stay right around the weight I was when I left the Army, but I didn't make any real effort to stay in good physical shape. And then something strange happened.

Biologists call it "Your Forties." Symptoms of "Your Forties" include things like your metabolism turning to crap. That well-oiled machine that at one time would process Oreos and bourbon with ease will now turn a carrot stick into a love handle just to screw with you.

I remember the moment when I realized that "Your Forties" had arrived. I had just finished what we refer to as the "long session" in the Virginia General Assembly. This is our sixty-day legislative session, which starts in January. During this time, you do a lot of sitting, talking, and eating. It is very fertile soil for "Your Forties" to exhibit its full fat-making potential.

In previous years, the fat I gained during the session, which I affectionately called my "session baby," quickly dissipated in the face of some pretty basic yard work.

Not this time.

So, I was faced with a choice. This was either going to be the new normal, where I was going to get progressively fatter and my wife would have to give me mercy sex for the rest of her life under the "for better or worse" clause of our wedding vows, or I was going to need to change some of my habits.

I decided to do a ninety-day gym program. I was going to stick to that program as closely as I could and see what happened. I went through the typical, showing up motivated, to about week 4, where I hoped an urgent call would force me to skip leg day to attend to important business. But I did stick with it long enough to do two things.

1. See results.

2. Make it a part of my routine.

I'm not claiming I love the gym, but I do love feeling stronger and more capable. It turns out that lifting is good not only for the body but also for the mind, diet, confidence, and everything else.

Now, based on the language I've used in this chapter, there will inevitably be people who suggest I am being "harsh" or "fat-phobic."

That is correct, because this book is for men.

One of my favorite memes on the planet illustrates the difference between how men and women approach this issue. It shows a picture of a woman asking her friend if she is fat, and her friend responding by telling her how gorgeous she is! Below is a guy asking his friend if he is fat, and his friend responds by saying, "I know four fat guys, and you're three of 'em."

Generally speaking, women need encouragement, and men need to feel capable. We motivate differently. It is what it is. So, get off your fat rear and get to the gym. You may not end up with a six-pack. But you'll thank me . . . especially after your wife thanks you first.

Get in shape, eat right, and make it a habit, not a fad, in your life. I chose a ninety-day gym program to start with. I pledge to go at least three times a week. I now go five. It has become part of my daily routine, and I actually miss it when I can't go.

As far as diet, I eat more red meat than any doctor would probably advise. I didn't cut out the things I loved the most; I significantly reduced overprocessed crap. I avoid fast food, and I don't overindulge in sweets. Notice I didn't say I never go to McDonald's or eat sugar anymore; I am just more aware. Your body can be trained through diet as well as exercise. Eat less crap, and you will stop craving it as much. But get started with someone, look for accountability, and pledge to stick with something until it becomes a habit. You won't regret it.

LESSON 10

HOW TO RUN FOR PUBLIC OFFICE

1. Pick a winnable office.

2. Have a ton of money or a lot of name recognition . . . preferably both.

3. Get really good at fundraising.

Those probably weren't the steps you were expecting. But the title of the chapter is HOW to run . . . not who should run, and those three steps are the easiest way to run for public office. You can have the best messaging, greatest arguments, incredible background, and relevant experience, but you will most likely lose to someone who's mastered the three things above.

Now, having said that, I can confess that the first time I ran for office, I arguably had none of those things . . . and yet I won.

"Nick, you should run for office!"

Well, screw you too. That's what I probably should have said. Instead, I ended up taking it seriously and eventually got elected to the Virginia House of Delegates.

Not the first time I was told that, mind you. You learn really quick in politics that it's not hard to find a nice lady who will tell a young person, "You should run for office!" Usually, it's because they are just thrilled that someone under the age of sixty-five is bothering to show up to a political event.

I blame my mother. She was the first one to introduce me to the world of politics, and as a young kid, it was exciting to hang out with people who were elected officials, party leaders, and decision-makers. There was a lot of talk about country, patriotism, freedom, civic responsibility, and making a difference.

Getting pictures with state representatives, congressmen, the governor: All of it made you feel like you were a part of not only something bigger than yourself but something with a direct line back to names like Washington, Jefferson, and Madison. It was a legacy as well as a connection with the past that gave you a sense of belonging and duty. As President Ronald Reagan said, "Freedom is never more than one generation away from extinction." Well, it wasn't going to be on my watch; I was going to serve, fight for, and preserve freedom for the next generation. I was not going to let the Gipper down!

And now, after multiple campaigns, ten years in a state legislature, hundreds of pieces of legislation, thousands of votes, floor speeches, debates, fundraisers, bill signings, parades, phone calls, receptions, and bad chicken dinners, I'll tell you: Reagan was right. The tenuous nature of freedom in our system of government requires the participation and ultimately oversight of the citizenry. The problem is understanding the nature of government itself.

America is not primarily a "democracy." And I don't just mean that in the sense that we are actually a constitutional republic that utilizes democratic processes to adjudicate differences with respect to representation and the adoption of laws.

I mean, the defining attribute of America was never meant to be the legal right to elect politicians every two, four, and six years. That's a component of our governmental system, and an important one. But the philosophical principle that defined this incredible experiment we call the United States of America was articulated in the Declaration of Independence.

"We hold these truths to be self-evident. That all men are created equal and endowed by their creator with certain unalienable rights. That among these are life, liberty, and the pursuit of happiness."

We hear these words now and take them as foregone conclusions at best, or a stinging indictment of our nation's inability to sufficiently live up to them at worst.

What we probably should do is stand in awe at the conquest ethic reigning supreme, especially during a time in history where slavery was rampant. The only "self-evident truth" to the vast majority of governments was that the ability to impose one's will was sufficient justification for the wielding of supreme executive power.

The unmitigated arrogance of today's professors, student activists, and political hacks casually dismissing and denigrating the incredible struggles of those who came before them is probably the single greatest indictment of so-called higher education in this country.

The bottom line is the United States is special, unique, and dare I say "exceptional" not because our history is perfect but because our founding creed was rooted in the idea that all human beings have inherent value and rights, granted to them by God, and that the primary responsibility of government was to preserve those rights so that its citizens could pursue happiness in accordance with THEIR definition, just so long as they did not infringe on the rights of others to do the same.

Here's the catch.

That only works if people believe it. It's only sustained if people demand it. And long ago, politicians discovered ways to bribe people out of their freedom for the promise of comfort or security.

John Adams said it best. "Our constitution was written for a moral and religious people and is totally unsuited to any other."

Atheists don't like that. I don't particularly care. Because he has been proved correct. Ultimately, the Declaration of Independence and the Constitution of the United States were never the safeguards of the people's freedom. The people themselves are. And atheists and nihilists don't have the best track record when it comes to building and preserving societies that will insist upon and fight for the preservation of freedom within a society where our rights are "unalienable" because they're from God.

So how do we preserve it? Well, it takes men who believe in it. But it also takes men who are willing to do the practical things necessary to run for office and win without surrendering their integrity.

So, understand your district, do what you need to gain the name recognition or wealth necessary to run, and be prepared to do a lot of things you don't particularly enjoy (like fundraising) to ensure that you can win on election day.

And now here is the hardest part for many. Know what vote you are willing to lose your seat over. Because I can assure you of this much, if you don't know what issue, vote, or action you are willing to lose it all for, then you don't belong there.

Compromise is an important factor in politics, but only to a point. If you don't know what you're willing to lose it all for, then the answer is nothing. The last thing we need in political office is more people who are great at getting elected but worthless when it comes to standing for what is right, especially when you have to do it alone.

LESSON 11

HOW TO DRINK WINE

1. Try different kinds of wine to figure out what you like.

2. Store it properly.

3. Don't try to look cooler than you are. If you don't know anything, ask questions.

4. Trust your palate. It's all subjective.

Step 1: Get a bourbon instead.

Okay, I agree with that, but knowing the basics of how to select and appreciate wine is not a horrible thing for a guy to know. I'm not saying that you have to be a sommelier or anything, but understanding a few basics about wine, the process of making it, basic pairing, and the proper way to smell, taste, and hold your wineglass does add a hint of sophistication to the guy who just read about how to kick in a door.

There are basically nine styles of wine, and if this book were about wine, we would go in-depth into all of them. But it isn't, so we aren't. Wines are generally categorized by color, body, and sweetness.

Color. Whites, reds, and rosés (think of rosé as in between white and red).

Body. Light, medium, or full. Basically, does it feel heavy? Usually more intense in flavor and with a higher alcohol content. Others will describe it as "mouth-filling." So, if you want to walk right into a "that's what she said" joke, be my guest.

Sweetness. This refers to sugar content.

There are also categories like aromatic for wines that give off strong aromas. And descriptions like oaked for wines that have been in contact with oak, such as those stored in an oak (often French oak) barrel.

Finally, there are also sparkling or fortified wines. Champagne is technically a sparkling wine that comes from the Champagne region of France. Sparkling wine from Spain is a Cava, and from Italy, Prosecco. Fortified wines have more alcohol in them (15–22%). This is done to increase the longevity of the wine. Common fortified wines are Port (Portugal) and Sherry (Spain).

You may also be well acquainted with the fortified wine brands of Thunderbird or MD 20/20, but we will not be covering any wines that come with a screw-off cap in this book.

White wines are usually made from white grapes . . . shocker. Your standard white wines include Riesling, Pinot Gris, Sauvignon Blanc, and Chardonnay.

Red wines are made from black grapes. Your standard red wines include Cabernet Sauvignon, Merlot, Syrah, and Zinfandel.

Generally speaking, your white wines are lighter and are paired with lighter fare such as seafood, poultry, and milder cheeses. By contrast, red wines are often paired with beef, lamb, smoked meats, and harder or more pungent cheeses.

My favorite wines are reds, specifically Cabernet Sauvignon, Barbera, and certain red blends. Octagon from Barboursville Winery in Orange County, Virginia, is excellent. In fact, if you have to purchase wine as a gift, a blended red from a specific vineyard is the easiest route. Wineries usually calibrate the blend to be the best representation of what they do, created to appeal to all drinkers.

What about age? Lighter white wines should actually be enjoyed within a couple of years. Many red wines, especially those higher in acidity and tannins, are ideal for aging. Aging a wine can help mellow the wine and allow it to develop a more robust aroma and taste. Aging includes a variety of factors, such as managing temperature, light, and humidity, as well as storing the bottle on its side and keeping it still. Sitting in the bottom of your dad's liquor cabinet for a few years doesn't count.

How to smell wine: "Nosing" the wine includes swirling the wine in the glass, then bringing the glass to your nose and breathing deeply (not too deeply) through the nose. Now, if you really want to look professional, you apply the five S's. See, swirl, smell, sip, and savor.

A quick note on the sommelier bringing you a tiny taste of wine when you get a bottle in a restaurant. They are not bringing it to you to watch you do the five S's. They don't care. They are asking you to verify that it has not gone bad. It's exactly the same as your wife asking you to smell the milk in the fridge. If they show you the bottle, it's for you to verify that it is the wine you ordered. If it *has* gone bad—usually musty smelling from cork taint—you will know it. Otherwise, pronounce it fine and allow them to pour it for everyone else.

See involves observing the coloring of the wine, which can help with determining age. Swirl helps release the aromas of the wine and indicates the alcohol level in the wine by the "legs," or little lines cascading down the interior of the glass after swirling. Smell is trying to identify different aromas. Then there is sip and savor. Savor includes allowing the wine to coat your mouth and tongue to appreciate the variety of flavors.

How to hold your wineglass: Thumb, pointer, and middle finger grasp the stem, with your other two fingers resting on the base of the glass. This helps keep the wine at the proper temperature and prevents your fingerprints from getting all over the glass, you savage.

How to pour wine: When it comes to "the pour," it's one-third the glass for red, one-half for white, and three-quarters for sparkling. Unless you're drinking wine alone . . . then you can just put the straw directly in the bottle while crying, you loser.

Don't feel intimidated, though. Even the guys who sometimes rate $5,000 bottles of wine consume a lot of Bud Light and Coke Zero the rest of the time.

If you have never really tried wine, I highly recommend going to a winery and doing a tasting. Some wineries can be a little bougie, but there are any number of nice, family-owned wineries where you can ask as many stupid questions as you would like, and they are happy to answer. I know, I've done it.

> Tip: While I prefer red to white wines, red wines will turn your teeth red and are more likely to stain if you spill them, so remember that if you are at a party.

LESSON

HOW TO DRINK WHISKEY

Now that you have graduated to whiskey, let's walk you through a similar overview of this superior beverage.

Whiskey is the common term for distilled, barrel-aged liquor made from fermented grains, usually corn, wheat, or rye in North America and barley in Ireland and Scotland. (Note that Scottish, Japanese, and Canadian whisky is spelled without the "e." Same beverage.)

Bourbon versus whiskey. All bourbons are whiskeys, but not all whiskeys are bourbons. Bourbon has certain geographical, content, and preparation criteria. It must be at least 51 percent corn, aged in new charred oak barrels, and made in the United States of America.

How to taste whiskey: There are four steps to tasting whiskey. Observe, smell, taste, and then, surprisingly enough, add a drop or two of water and taste again.

The observe stage, just like in tasting wine, is to appreciate the color of the whiskey. Like wine, the color can inform you about the age of the whiskey, with older whiskeys typically being darker, although other things can affect that. To smell the whiskey, bring it up to your nose slowly, and don't inhale deeply initially, as whiskeys with higher alcohol content can shock your senses. When you take your first sip, make it a small one and try to focus on the flavors. Just like with wine, let it coat the mouth and tongue. The fourth step of adding water is optional, but you will be surprised by what adding just a couple of drops of water does to open up the flavor of a whiskey.

My favorite sipping whiskey is Uncle Nearest 1856, which is a Tennessee whiskey and technically a bourbon, but Tennesseans, being the rebellious type, decided that they would call it what they wanted.

My favorite bourbon or Tennessee whiskey–based drink is a smoked Old Fashioned, which is a cube or sphere of ice, two ounces of the bourbon of your choice, three dashes of bitters, a pinch of raw sugar (or one-half ounce of simple syrup), a Maraschino cherry, the smoke of your choice, and garnish with an orange peel. (I use some zest from the orange in the drink as well.) You can buy a very nice, customized travel cocktail smoker from Hidden Labs on Instagram.

Whiskey pairs well with grilled meats, strong cheeses, some desserts, barbecue, stress, anger, sadness, joy, Tuesdays . . . well, pretty much all days, you get the point.

There is a website called "Aged and Charred" that can walk you through the nine types of whiskey and the descriptions.

> Tip 1: Ordering your drink "neat" means without any ice or mixer. "On the rocks" means with ice. Ideally, the ice for a whiskey-based drink includes a single cube or ice sphere. Don't expect that for "Jack and Coke," though.
>
> Tip 2: Ordering whiskey and Coke may attract ridicule, but if everyone else at the poker table is drinking it straight, you can switch to just Coke at some point in the evening and take them for everything. The more you know.

LESSON

HOW TO HAVE GREAT SEX

1. Find one woman you love and marry her.

2. Have sex only with her.

3. Practice as much as feasible.

"All the top G's in history had harems."

That statement isn't incorrect. It's just incomplete. When you read history a little more closely, you discover that harems were a huge source of social upheaval, leading to intrigue, rebellion, and even fratricide. Regimes that weathered sickness, famine, and war have fallen to lust.

Watch a little of what has become affectionately known as the "manosphere" on social media, and you will probably come across a physically fit, financially successful, intelligent, and articulate middle-aged man telling younger men that body counts are a bad thing for a woman, but it's "different" for a man.

Again. Not wrong, just incomplete.

Just so we're clear, unlike in combat, "body count" means how many people you've had sex with.

And it turns out body counts matter for both men and women, and high ones are bad for both men and women. But it affects them in different ways.

Serving in the military, and specifically in Special Forces, I was something of an anomaly, having only ever been with my wife. And by "anomaly," I mean I think I only ever encountered one other person in SF with a similar experience.

SF guys, in general, are usually physically fit and competent. The fact that we are Americans also means that we are rich by world standards, and since we spend a lot of time in countries with beautiful women and a very low GDP per capita rate, SF guys tend to be kind of popular.

There was something of a joke that if you saw an average-looking SF guy with a gorgeous Thai or Korean girlfriend . . . 1st Group. Eastern European? 10th Group. Panamanian or Colombian? That would be the 7th Group, and so on, based on the geographical region their group covered down on.

So why do I point this out?

Because I have seen what happens when guys get the idea that having a lot of sex with numerous anonymous women, both in the US and overseas, is "no big deal," simply "part of the culture" or "just what guys do."

It sets up a mindset that is very difficult for guys to break when they do get married, because instead of sex being something unique and special to be shared with a woman they love, it's just a physical act engaged in for self-gratification or street cred.

Now look, I've heard all the biological arguments based on the assumption that human beings are little more than slightly more evolved animals. The argument is that because lions, chimps, or even dolphins all engage in rampant promiscuity, we should see ourselves as free to do the same, since we all are mammals. The thing is, that argument breaks down pretty quickly when you start asking people if we should adopt the other mating rituals found in the wild, because last I checked, most males in the animal kingdom don't ask permission before satisfying their sexual urges. So, do you really want humans to act like nothing more than animals, or would you like to apply a higher level of morality to the interaction?

The simplest explanation for monogamy would be the biblical one, where it clearly lays out that sex is supposed to be between a man and a woman within the confines of marriage.

On a more practical level, I can assure you that a good woman, the kind of beautiful, intelligent, nurturing woman you want for a wife and mother to your children, doesn't stay up at night dreaming about her brave, strong knight in shining armor, banging every maiden he can talk into bed. The kind of woman who has "no problem" with your high body count is probably not being honest . . . either about what she's really after or about her own body count.

There is the question of quality. Whenever I hear someone say, "It's just sex," I automatically think, "Well, that person probably sucks at it."

Sex shouldn't be "casual"; it should be awesome. Do you think you are more likely to have "great sex" with some rando who was probably doing the same thing with some other guy last Friday, or a woman you are so completely in love with that you are ready to spend the rest of your life with?

Porn and smut novels have created a false and destructive impression of what conditions create "great sex." But talk to someone who has escaped the porn industry, and you discover that far from being exciting and exotic, you will find a lot of broken people struggling to find any real meaning or connection in their personal relationships.

Great sex includes passion, trust, attraction, communication, and commitment. You want to know that she is yours and yours alone. She wants to know the same thing about you. High body counts erode that trust. This is not to say that you can't overcome a checkered past, but better to avoid the mistakes in the first place.

An inability to pair-bond, being compared to some random dude she had sex with at a concert, or coming face-to-face with the real possibility that you are the guy she "settled for" when she realized that the other guys were happy to sleep with her but were never going to marry her. And if you spend your whole life in the same small town as all her old lovers, a Little League game crowd turns into a minefield.

A woman with a low, or preferably no, body count is ultimately important to a man for a host of practical and emotional reasons that men shouldn't have to be ashamed of. We don't trash women for wanting a man who can protect and provide; we shouldn't trash a man for wanting a woman who hasn't given herself to a bunch of other guys. But . . .

The same goes for guys.

Okay . . . let's consider that. First of all, it's fine to point out the areas of the animal kingdom you like when it comes to justifying your impulses, but closer examination suggests that we might not want to replace sexual ethics with Animal Planet. The lion might only have to defend the pride, eat, and have sex, but there are other species within the animal kingdom that consume their husbands shortly after having sex. Furthermore, sex in the wild tends to be a lot more "rapey." I'm assuming the people using the animal kingdom as their guide for sexual ethics don't insist on adopting all such practices.

Let's put it another way. Women tend to be more emotionally invested in sex than men are. Part of that is due to the biological realities of pregnancy that men don't have to contend with in the same way. Now you could use this as an argument for why women shouldn't sleep around and why it's okay for men . . . or you could come to the very logical conclusion that if you want to have the best sex possible with a woman, you should be the sort of guy she can emotionally connect with on the highest level possible. Which probably means you haven't been or aren't sleeping with a bunch of women she will now be comparing herself to.

Putting all your eggs in one basket, so to speak, solves another common problem. Late-night bar conversations and anonymous internet forums are filled with people asking, "How do I let my partner know I need more of this and that in bed?" The correct answer is: If you do not know this person well enough to have that conversation, you do not know them well enough to be having sex with them.

Great sex is part of a great relationship. Bottom line, I think Scripture just got it right . . . again. Both men and women are, for emotional, physical, biological, practical, and spiritual reasons, supposed to save sex for within the confines of a marriage between a man and a woman. The reason being, you avoid all of the problems that potentially arise from premarital sex, and you place sex on the pedestal it deserves to be on.

By treating sex as a wonderful and sacred thing between two people committed to one another, you can experience it the way it was meant to be. By contrast, whenever I hear someone talk about how much fun "casual sex" is, I instantly think, "You and I must have different definitions because if it were that great, *casual* would not be the word you would use to describe sex."

LESSON 14

HOW TO WIN A FIGHT

"I can take an ass whipping."

"Good, because I can give one."

That was what the head of our combatives training in the Special Forces Qualification Course told us as his opening. The thing is, he didn't carry himself like some kind of "in your face" jackass. If you saw him at a bar, you probably wouldn't have assumed that he was one of the more dangerous guys there. I mean . . . until you popped off, and then you would have found out pretty quick.

I also distinctly remember him asking us: As Green Berets, was it more important to know how to fight or quote Shakespeare? We all said fight . . . he then acted like he was pointing a gun at us and said, "Quote Shakespeare." His point being, you never know what kind of capability you might need in a given situation, and his job was to make us more capable in a particular field, but that wasn't an excuse to ignore the others.

Now, if I'm being honest, I thought the example he chose was kind of stupid, but the point was still well taken.

So, look, when I say you should know how to fight, I'm not saying you need to be octagon-ready at any given time. I'm not saying you should be the guy looking for trouble. I'm simply pointing out that as a man, and especially as a husband and father, you may find yourself in a situation where you need to be able to fight on someone else's behalf. Can you imagine how you would feel if your wife or child was in danger, and you didn't possess a basic ability to defend them from physical harm?

I've met men before who were certainly "willing to fight," and that's certainly necessary. The will to do something is incredibly important. I'm willing to hit cleanup for the Dodgers . . . but something tells me my complete lack of capability is going to prevent me from getting a contract anytime soon.

If it makes you feel better, tell yourself that "if the situation ever arose, I would die for my family." Well, good for you. Now, if it came to that, I'd rather kill the guy trying to hurt them than die for them, but you do you. Because let's face it, if you're willing to fight for your family, but incapable of it, then dying, or at least getting your ass kicked, is exactly what you plan to do.

A man who says he is willing to fight to defend his family may possess the will, but if he doesn't possess the capability, then I guess your family gets to look on in horror as they lose you, and then the bad guy does whatever he wants to them next.

Staying in shape is important, lifting is important, but knowing at least the basics of fighting is right up there with the rest if you want to be a man.

I could give you plenty of good advice directly on how to win a fight. Use knees and elbows. Don't risk breaking every bone in your fingers. Be fast and aggressive. Don't square up and wait like in the movies. Go for vulnerable areas like the eyes, throat, and groin. Try to stay balanced and off the ground.

But if you're serious about this, and you should be, you need to work on it. With professionals.

Brazilian Jiu-Jitsu, boxing, wrestling, Krav Maga, whatever you prefer. As long as it has a good mix of striking and grappling, not only will it be a great workout, but it will also equip you with a useful capability and an incredible amount of confidence.

> You will be shocked at how minimal, consistent training will make you more formidable in a fight. Combative training just a couple of times a week will make you more prepared for a fight than probably 99 percent of the population. Not simply because you will have a better grasp of technique, but because you will have developed your fight-or-flight instinct that will equip you to react the way you want to and the way your family may need you to in a difficult situation.

LESSON 15

HOW TO PICK THE "RIGHT WOMAN"

1. Faith and principles first (deal-breakers).

2. Similar expectations and goals for marriage and life (could be deal-breakers).

3. Similar hobbies and interests (nice to have, but not deal-breakers).

4. Physical attraction (important, but not more important than the first two).

I'm married to a hot blond who has given me a great life and wonderful children.

I got married young. Nineteen to be exact. I'm not telling you to get married young; that's just when I did.

My wife and I have been married for over twenty-five years, have three kids, two of whom are adults, and I can honestly say, I love her more now than the day I married her. If I had to do it all over again, I wouldn't hesitate.

I've had people hear that and tell me, "That's sweet." They are happy for me, but they think we just got "lucky."

Oh . . . is that what it was?

Let's be honest and acknowledge that often in life, we are the beneficiaries of things beyond our control. Decisions that we had nothing to do with conferred some sort of advantage that others might not have had. Maybe you call that "luck," maybe you call it "blessed," but everyone at some point has experienced it.

But here is what I've noticed. People chalking up the success of others to "luck" are usually more interested in excusing their own failures than they are in listening to what worked. Because let's face it, the plans that work usually require hard work, discipline, and sacrifice. Chalking everything up to "luck" might not get you what you really want, but at least it absolves you of responsibility.

There is no doubt that there were any number of factors that made meeting my wife when I did fortuitous and that I had nothing to do with. So what? You know what does matter? The decisions we did make, regardless of how much control we had over the circumstances we found ourselves in.

So, if you're not interested in how a young couple, who both came from broken homes, went into a profession with one of the highest divorce rates, overcame a multitude of stressful situations and circumstances involving money and moving and war, only to build something that both of them are incredibly happy with, then by all means, dismiss it as luck, and move along.

But if you are curious . . . here is how it started.

I was a freshman in high school when I first met my wife. I distinctly remember looking at her and saying to myself, "Well, that's never going to happen." And I was right for the next three years. But my senior year, things changed. For some reason, she decided she liked me. I don't know if it was my charm, intelligence, or maybe the fact that we had a graduating class of only twenty-seven, but whatever it was, I was going to exploit the hell out of it!

But here is the real question: Aside from her being smoking hot, how did I know she was "the one"? I've thought a lot about this. Namely, the things we did right and the things we did wrong, but there were a few things that really stood out.

Principles Matter: I don't care how hot she is; if you don't have the same core principles, it isn't going to last. That's because everything—interests, goals, looks—changes over time, sometimes drastically. Core fundamental principles are far more likely to shape major decisions in your roles within the marriage and if raising kids. Tina and I shared the same faith, but we had long discussions about what Christianity meant to us. It formed the basis of our worldview on important topics like truth, love, and justice.

We also both saw it as authoritative, so that even though I was the "head of the household," there was still an objective truth and morality that governed my actions and responsibilities, and the same for her. I cannot emphasize enough how important this is if you have fundamental differences with respect to how you judge morality and choose life priorities. Good luck trying to keep your marriage intact while navigating a difficult world that is not always keen to assist.

Sometimes people will ask me, How do you increase your odds of finding someone with shared principles? The answer in many cases is "where you meet them matters." Many of the places people go to meet a potential love interest revolve around fun, dancing, conversation, drinking, and other activities, which may be fine in and of themselves, but they either convey nothing about principles or they convey the opposite of what you want. If you want to increase your odds of meeting someone with shared principles, you should spend time in places and with organizations that revolve around them. Church comes to mind.

Goals and Expectations Matter: Not as much as principles, but it's very important to discuss them. Especially on the most important questions, such as the roles you will play as husband and wife, and hopefully one day as mother and father. Tina and I spoke about these things extensively. It was actually fun to discuss. Did she want to work outside the home? How much should I make? Did I see it as my job to be the primary breadwinner? How many kids would you like to have? Dogs or cats? This is important because a wonderful person who shares your values but has drastically different goals in life might be the makings of a good friendship, but not a good marriage. Better to find out sooner rather than later.

Hobbies and Interests Matter: Not as much as goals, but they do provide an indication of whether you have much in common. The good news is a lot of people usually meet around shared interests, so the question is often answered, at least in part, all by itself. But don't confuse shared interests with a genuine connection. People often meet in the context of an activity they enjoy, perhaps a job or project they are working on, and confuse the connection around a shared interest with an actual relationship. And then they find out that when the project is over, so is the connection.

Also, be willing to allow your interests to adapt over time. If you had told me when I was a twenty-four-year-old Green Beret that one day I would enjoy gardening or cooking, I probably would have told you that you were crazy, but I have spent a lot of time and money trying to get my seed starts just right!

Physical Attraction Matters: It's also probably the most likely thing to screw up your whole process and get both of you into a marriage you shouldn't be in. The reason I say that is as a man, especially, physical attraction is a powerful motivator. If you allow attraction to tempt you to get physical too fast, you will ignore important questions about principles, goals, and interests in order to satisfy your newfound desire to have sex with this hot woman you like.

This is not about denying you something you want; it's about delayed gratification to get something so much better. This is also about growing with one woman over the years whose beauty will be enhanced because of the memories, challenges, and triumphs together. It's about achieving a kind of genuine passion for a woman, which enhances her physical beauty and keeps your connection strong throughout your years together.

LESSON

HOW TO PIT A CAR

1. First, determine whether you really need to do this . . . "it will look cool" is not actually sufficient reasoning according to most state laws (and you thought you lived in a free country).

2. Bring your vehicle up to the rear quarter panel of the target vehicle while maintaining speed.

3. Make contact with the target vehicle.

4. Accelerate while turning into the target vehicle.

5. As the rear of the target vehicle begins to move to the side you are pushing, turn the steering wheel to where the front of your vehicle is pushing the rear quarter panel of the vehicle you are chasing.

6. Straighten out and accelerate through, causing the target vehicle to flip around (while remaining on the ground), with the front of the vehicle you were chasing now facing in the opposite direction and causing the engine to stall.

7. Be ready to either position your vehicle in such a way as to give chase or leave the vehicle to pursue on foot if they make a run for it.

If another man ever asks you, "Why would anyone need to know how to pit a car?," that is not good friend material. I'm telling you, you don't need that kind of negativity in your life. There are literally dozens of good reasons why this is a useful skill and probably hundreds why it's just awesome.

PIT is an acronym that stands for Precision Immobilization Technique, not a slang term for trying to drive someone into a "pit." I can't believe you thought that's what it meant. I know I didn't when I first heard it. Anyway . . .

One of the best times I ever had in the military was attending Gryphon Group's driving course. Remember all the totally awesome answers to your driving instructor's questions that he told you were "wrong" or "illegal" or "highly dangerous?" Well, get ready to be vindicated, because at Gryphon Group, those answers are probably still wrong, but Gryphon likes where your mind is at.

While I usually despise government spending, I'm not going to lie. I have never had that much fun utilizing tax dollars for a good and noble purpose. Namely, getting in high-speed chases and shooting people with paintballs.

Among the many skills taught at this course, which included shooting through windshields, was the time-honored tradition of causing a car to spin out and stall. I know you were probably thinking spin out and do three flips (which is possible), but in reality, that isn't what you're going for. That can cause a lot more damage to both the vehicle and the contents within.

A well-executed PIT is when a car is ever so gently nudged in such a way that it does a 180-degree spin while remaining on the ground, thus causing it to stop moving. When done correctly, the vehicle is not destroyed, and no serious injuries are sustained by the people in either car or innocent bystanders.

It's not as easy to pull off as you may think, since the person driving the other car usually fails to cooperate. They drive erratically, change lanes, speed up, slow down, and any number of other maneuvers that can make it difficult to get into position to execute the PIT.

So here's how to perform a PIT in a few easy steps.

1. **Pacing:** You want to match pace with the target vehicle, offsetting to either the left or the right. Ideally, you want to line up in such a way that gives you more room to maneuver and allows the target car to flip around.

2. **Positioning:** Accelerate to where the front quarter panel of your car is about even with the rear quarter panel of the target vehicle.

3. **Contact:** Slowly turn into the rear quarter panel of the target vehicle and make contact.

4. **Push:** Once contact has been achieved, turn toward the target vehicle at about a quarter turn of your steering wheel, pushing the rear quarter panel, as if you were trying to push the target vehicle horizontal with your own.

5. **Straighten:** Once the target vehicle starts to spin, straighten your own vehicle to assist in pushing the target car completely around.

6. **Position:** Once the target vehicle has been stalled out, you should position your own car to barricade or prevent egress.

> Tip: Remember that just because a car has been successfully pitted doesn't mean that it's completely inoperable. Ideally this maneuver is done with other chase cars to help barricade the target vehicle once the maneuver has been completed.

To answer the question of the guy who is no longer your friend, some of the practical reasons you might do this include an out-of-control vehicle that has lost its brakes, a driver who has passed out or died behind the wheel of a car that is causing damage to others, or perhaps that one douchebag who keeps skipping in and out of lanes with a "Tolerance" bumper sticker . . . okay, maybe not that last one. But it will feel good to know you could do it if you needed to. Believe me.

LESSON 17

HOW TO NEVER HAVE TO SLEEP ON THE COUCH

1. Your wife's happiness matters.

2. So does yours.

3. Neither of you will be happy in a relationship where you always placate one another instead of achieving actual resolution and unity.

"Happy wife, happy life" is one of those cheap little sayings that I've really come to despise, because it seems plausible, but actually has horrible implications. Don't get me wrong, I want my wife to be happy, but if your relationship with your wife is primarily motivated by avoiding conflict to "make her happy," you're doing it wrong.

Now, I can already hear the response: "But women bring up old crap. They don't use logic. They get too emotional. It's just easier to let it go to keep the peace."

If you are just giving your wife what she wants, or are avoiding taking on serious issues, because you think it will result in a fight, then you're contributing to the very conditions you're complaining about. You aren't providing "genuine happiness." You're just placating her. You're treating her the same way a crappy parent treats a petulant toddler every time the child throws a temper tantrum. Spoiler alert: People respond to incentives. They tend to respond in whatever way they think will get them the best result. And there is nothing more pathetic in a marriage than when both sides are responding in shallow and petty ways because they have both become convinced that that is the best they can get.

The wife wants a relationship, but she gets placated. The husband wants peace, but he gets a temporary ceasefire, purchased at the price of the genuine article.

Look, guys. There is a reason that the world's bestselling book, the Bible, has several verses dedicated to avoiding contentious women. But keep in mind that while some women may be born contentious, most are made that way. Often, as a result of being physically unable to impose their will, they are forced to develop other techniques to achieve their objectives. And this sort of thing isn't limited to women.

Both men and women have traits that can manifest themselves in negative or positive ways. So, how do you get the positive traits to come through instead of the negative? Reward the positive.

This goes for both spouses, by the way. It's not the husband's job to eternally reward the good in the hope that one day it will be reciprocated. Wives need to do it as well. If they refuse, husbands shouldn't put up with that. That doesn't mean leaving, walking away, or "being in the doghouse." It means fighting for your marriage by insisting on discussing issues in a reasonable way and with the mindset of improving the marriage.

In twenty-five years of marriage, there has been only one time when my wife told me she wanted me to sleep in a different room for the night. I refused. I wasn't going to be pushed out of OUR bed. So, we hashed it out. And I ended up needing to apologize. That's right, not because I wanted to go back to my room. I already had that. I apologized because, as we discussed her feelings and the reasons behind them, it turned out I had said things and behaved in ways that made her feel isolated.

So, guys, remember something. Standing your ground is a good thing, just as long as you remember that standing your ground means talking it out, actively listening, and potentially having to apologize, NOT because you're tired of the argument or because you don't want to sleep on the couch. If you're the sort of man who gets banished to the couch, grab your pillow, blankets, and balls, and remind your wife that you are in this marriage for life. If there is something that's problematic, then it needs to be discussed right now. You don't want there to be a single night where the two of you can't stand to be beside one another.

Look, I get it that sometimes people need to cool down before they say or do something stupid. But honestly, there is a reason that the Bible says not to sleep on your anger. Cooling down or processing is fine, but unless the cops need to be called, a man should not be banished from his bed. But remember that women are typically the more vulnerable ones in the relationship, so put your wife at ease and let her know that there is no problem you two can't figure out together.

LESSON 18

HOW TO TEACH YOUR KIDS TO SHOOT

Teaching your kids the proper care and handling of a firearm is actually one of the best ways to ensure that they don't get hurt by one. While the statistics suggesting that firearms are the number one killer of children are heavily manipulated for political purposes, firearms can pose a threat to kids if they are not taught proper respect for guns.

Some of my earliest memories are of going into my grandfather's den and listening to him tell stories while he smoked his pipe. My grandfather decorated primarily with pictures and guns. He had an authentic version of a rifle used in every major war or conflict the United States had been in from the Revolution through the Korean War. He taught me about the history and how to properly handle firearms. I have pictures of me in my feet pajamas holding a Thompson submachine gun with a one-hundred-round magazine.

I probably fired my first firearm around five or six years old. At fourteen, I was assembling and disassembling one of his Colt 1911s blindfolded as he threw out parts from other pistols . . . good times. But what I remember most, without being able to describe a specific moment or starting point, was the emphasis on safety. It was deeply ingrained that handling a firearm was a great responsibility. A man handled a firearm with skill and respect. To do otherwise was tantamount to not being a real man.

I conveyed this to my own children, both my son and my daughters. It began with showing them firearms at a young age and making sure that they knew they were never allowed to touch them unless it was under the direct supervision of Dad or Mom. Getting to hold the firearm was a great privilege and demonstration of trust that they would lose immediately if they ever broke the rules.

When we shot with friends on our property, they got to participate as young as five or six, just like I did. Getting to shoot was a rite of passage, and while we would of course praise them for the accuracy when they shot, we were always intentional about praising them first and foremost for their maturity and safety. The results were what you might expect.

It turns out that children like to participate in events with adults. To be trusted with an important job or task gives them an opportunity to demonstrate that they belong there. It is something that must be earned, and so it has value. We have a natural incentive to protect things of value and therefore self-regulate.

To sum up . . .

1. Expose your children to firearms first by allowing them to be present when preparing to shoot and then shooting. Teach them that firearms are to be respected because they are important tools, but they are also dangerous.

2. Set clear guidelines for when your child can hold a firearm and the consequences for touching one without your permission or direct supervision.

3. When shooting, invite them to participate under your direct supervision, teaching them the proper way to hold, aim, and shoot. Praise them for their safety, and then for accuracy. They need to prioritize safety over being a "good shot."

4. Teach them the proper process for loading and unloading, and how to deal with a malfunction. When young, they are to keep the gun pointed at the target or the ground in front of them and to ask for assistance. As they get older, they can be taught how to correct the malfunction and continue shooting.

5. Teach them how to disassemble and clean the firearm.

6. Once these skills have been mastered, you can teach things like cancel carry, drawing, engaging, multiple targets, and other skills.

NOTE: At some point, a younger shooter will probably do something that is unsafe, even if it is very minor. You cannot excuse this. The best way to instill a serious attention to detail with respect to safety is to enforce the safety rules. You violate the rules, you are called out, disciplined, and must immediately stop shooting. I know there are some things that you may "let slide" when someone is young, but this isn't the area to do this. They have to believe you're serious.

When your kids get a little older, starting them out with a BB or pellet gun can be a good way to see if the safety rules you have put in place have been properly appreciated.

When my son was younger, we got him a pellet gun for his tenth birthday. As he was aiming to shoot, he saw out of the corner of his eye that his little sister had started to run in front of the firing line. She was far enough away that he would have had to have made a serious error to get anywhere close to where she was, but he immediately took his finger off the trigger and yelled at her, half in anger and half in fear. He was seriously worried that he could have hurt his sister. This demonstrated to me that he took this responsibility seriously.

We have now been shooting with our children for over sixteen years and have never once had a serious safety violation or ever had to worry about our children handling a firearm outside the boundaries provided. All our kids love to shoot, do it safely and well, and despise any politician who would seek to infringe on their Second Amendment rights.

LESSON 19

HOW TO HOT-WIRE A CAR

"Why would you ever need to hot-wire a car?"

Seriously, you need to get rid of the guy in your friend group who keeps asking these lame questions. Just like being able to pit a vehicle, there are, in fact, practical reasons why this is a useful skill. What if you find yourself getting chased by violent thugs in a foreign country? Or, what if you really want to impress a woman? What if that same woman you impressed steals your keys and throws them in the sewer because it turns out she's crazy? Now you can still drive home! Those are three really good reasons to know how to do this!

Look, I will gladly admit that you probably will never use this skill, but you will probably never have to apply a tourniquet on anyone, either. Doesn't mean it's not a good thing to know how to do.

Now, before we get started, understand that hot-wiring cars is actually getting a lot more difficult. It won't be too long before this is a skill that works only in foreign countries with an excess of older model vehicles. The modern version of this is how to "hack" the car, since it's increasingly becoming one big computer on wheels. But here goes . . .

The screwdriver/drill method: In some older vehicles, you can literally just shove a flathead screwdriver into the ignition and use enough force to break the locking pins and start the car by turning the screwdriver like you would a key. I kid you not. Thing is, this isn't really "hot-wiring," it's just bypassing the locking mechanism the key uses to engage the ignition. But still effective in some models. Again, this is probably NOT working on anything built in the twenty-first century.

Hot-wiring the steering column: Remove the plastic cover around the steering column to expose the access panels. Find the various bundles of wires. There will usually be wires that lead to column-mounted controls on either side. These bundles lead to things like lights, wipers, indicator lights, and other accessories. You're looking for the bundle that leads to the battery, ignition, and so on.

That bundle will usually include wires for the power supply for the ignition switch, the ignition wire, and the wire for the starter. Odds are the ignition wire will be brown, starter wire yellow, and battery wires red, but this CAN and does vary.

Strip enough of the plastic away from the battery wires to expose the metal and twist them together. Then connect the ignition on/off wire. At this point, you should see the dash lights and other electrical indicators come on.

To start the car, you will now need to spark the wire. Strip the plastic coating from the starter wire and touch the end to the connected battery wires. You don't need to connect that wire by twisting. You just need to tap it to get your spark. Keep in mind . . . the reason you are getting a spark is because that wire is live. Don't touch the exposed wire!

Once the engine starts, you can detach the starter wire. Don't immediately try to drive off. Rev the engine a few times to ensure that it isn't going to stall out. Also, remember that you may need to break the steering lock before driving anywhere, or this could be a short trip. You will probably be able to do that with the brute force of either turning the wheel or popping off the metal key whole.

To turn the car off, you just untwist the battery wires from the ignition wire, and the car will turn off.

There are other methods, but these are the ones that are common and don't require as much equipment.

A few things to keep in mind. If a car has a fob or a chip, none of this is probably working. Cars have become increasingly difficult to hot-wire, and for good reason. I would do a chapter on how to hack a car in an emergency situation, but I have no idea how to do that.

LESSON 20

HOW TO TALK ABOUT YOUR WIFE

"Man, my wife will not stop nagging me. Every day it's something else. She is driving me nuts."

Okay, sounds like you have an issue. Go fix it and then get back to me.

I honestly hate it when guys endlessly complain about their wives or marriage. I'm not talking about a guy who honestly needs to talk through something with someone they trust. I'm talking about a culture where, as soon as the guys get together, it's a nonstop wife-bashing contest.

Honestly, all it signals to me is that you suck at being a husband.

Now, before the guys get pissed at me, let me clarify something. Women tend to be just as bad, if not worse, at this. Speaking of their husbands as if they were idiots incapable of surviving without them.

So, let's acknowledge something up front. There is a significant difference between husbands and wives making stereotypical jokes about each other that can be appreciated by both, and running your spouse into the ground to your friends. The difference is usually between joking about quirks or stereotypes that both husbands and wives acknowledge and those that represent genuine problems or insecurities.

If you don't understand the difference, try kidding your wife in public about owning too many shoes. Then try telling everyone she wears a men's size twelve and see how that goes over.

Trashing your spouse to your friends should be seen as an admission of failure on your part, especially if you're bringing up issues only to people who you know will always take your side, even if you're the one being unreasonable or lazy.

When I would hear guys incessantly complaining about their wives, it didn't cause me to think their wives were crazy or difficult. It caused me to think that they were weak husbands.

Now, is it possible that a situation can become so exacerbated that they need to blow off steam with a trusted friend? Yes . . . within reason and under two conditions.

1. They really do want to solve the issue.

2. They are talking to someone who wants their marriage to succeed, not just take their boy's side in a fight.

I told my daughter and son-in-law when they were engaged that after they were married, the primary person they should go to if they had an issue was their spouse. I told my daughter that while I would always be there for her, no matter what, that if she ever needed to talk to me about an issue with her husband, and provided it wasn't an issue of abuse, then my job would be to give her advice to save the marriage, not simply "support her."

One of the greatest gifts my wife and I have given each other is that we build each other up to our friends and family; we don't tear each other down.

In fact, outside marriage, talking well of people behind their backs is a good idea. It's rare for anyone to think better of someone who has just let loose a litany of complaints.

> This one is pretty simple. Uplift your wife. This doesn't mean that you have to turn every casual conversation into a dissertation on how wonderful your wife is. It just means that you choose to have your wife's back no matter what and signify to others that you love her. You might actually be surprised at how it is appreciated when done in a sincere way. If it isn't, then understand that you may have some unhealthy friendships. A guy who doesn't mind constantly trashing his wife has some issues that probably affect more than just his marriage.

LESSON 21

HOW TO GET ALPHA MALES TO WORK TOGETHER

1. Shared mission keeps people focused on the task to be performed.

2. Shared hardship creates mutual respect.

3. Complementary skill sets create an environment where men can have their domain while respecting the skills of others.

4. Objective standards for excellence create mechanisms for men to earn respect.

5. Danger reminds people of the seriousness of their responsibilities to the mission and each other.

ODAs shouldn't work.
"What is an ODA?" I hear you asking, dear reader. An ODA is

an "Operational Detachment Alpha." Also known as an "A-Team," it is the basic operational unit of an Army Special Forces (Green Berets) element.

It consists of twelve personnel. A Captain who is the 18A and Team Leader. A 180A who is a Warrant Officer and the Executive Officer of the Team. An 18Z who is typically a Master Sergeant (SGT) and the Team SGT. Usually, the man with the most team time and Special Forces experience is on the team. A Sergeant First Class (SFC) as an 18F who is the intel SGT and then a Senior SFC and Junior Staff Sergeant (SSG) in the positions of 18B Weapons, 18C Engineer, 18D Medic, and 18E Communications.

What you usually discover about an SF ODA right away is that it tends to be filled with people who are physically fit, reasonably intelligent, professionally competent, sarcastic as hell, slow to suffer fools, highly competitive, and very meritocratic.

While it's true that the captain is in charge of the team, it's also true that a wise and discerning captain will lean heavily on his team sergeant for guidance and advice. Rank matters in SF, it just doesn't matter as much as being good at your job.

Special Forces is one of the few places in the military where you might see a lower-ranking, but more experienced, noncommissioned officer (NCO) politely ask an officer if he would like to remove his head from his ass, if said officer is doing something monumentally stupid.

An SF ODA is a curious cocktail of "toxic" masculinity, bourbon, and machine guns. The kind of thing a gender studies professor would despise.

It shouldn't work. Putting a bunch of A-type personalities on a team should lead to merciless infighting, jockeying for power, and mistrust.

In reality, it's probably one of the most effective and efficient military units in history, with people working together in some of the most unusual, austere, and challenging environments in military history and pulling off incredible successes where others might have thought it impossible with so few people.

So, if it shouldn't work, and yet it does . . . why? And what does it show us about men and missions?

Shared Mission: SF has seven core mission sets, but the ones that tend to be unique to Green Berets are Unconventional Warfare, Counterinsurgency, and Foreign Internal Defense. In short, we are either the insurgents fighting the government or assisting the government in fighting insurgents. But either way, we are working by, through, and with the local population, host nation forces, or local rebel groups. We have to rely on a mixture of diplomacy and combat effectiveness to function. Many of the missions are likely, if not guaranteed, to be dangerous. Failing to do one's job could cause someone else to get hurt.

Shared Training: All SF operators are expected to be "door kickers." I don't mean this in the way that some branches claim that "everyone is a rifleman." Regardless of what your specialty on the team is, everyone is expected to be able to shoot, move, and communicate effectively. It also provides areas of shared skill sets for which competition is healthy and expected.

Specialized Training: This is critical. Not everyone can be an expert at everything, so there needs to be specialization and focus. This not only ensures that the team will be able to do far more than it would if everyone were "just a competent rifleman" but also allows for highly competent people to have an area of responsibility that is uniquely theirs and on which the team depends. By providing responsibility, you also provide a mechanism for earning specialized respect and a purpose on the team that is uniquely yours.

Meritocracy: Rank doesn't get you nearly as far in SF as it might in other professions or even other areas of the military. You must be good at what you do. An SF soldier who relies on rank to deflect criticism will not last long. This reinforces that there is an objective set of standards by which you are judged, and if you meet them, you are considered a reliable member of the team regardless of your rank. Having objective standards that anyone can attain regardless of rank, seniority, or experience is important.

High Stakes: This doesn't just mean combat. It means a highly competitive environment where failure can mean everything from death to loss of face to the company going out of business. High-stakes environments provide both a level of motivation and need for discipline that other areas of life do not. As well as a mechanism for weeding out people who can't handle pressure.

You combine these attributes in an organization, and the result is highly motivated, disciplined, and trained individuals who feel like part of a team, know what is expected of them, receive respect for their competency in a specific field or function, and have respect for others in different yet complementary functions. They know their place and purpose, and they derive meaning from not only the mission they are given but the connections they have through shared sacrifice, danger, and purpose.

> I have been a member of several teams, organizations, groups, and companies since leaving SF. And I've always been struck by how well that military unit worked compared with others. The principles are universally relevant. If you want a successful organization, have a well-understood mission that people can believe in, common responsibilities that unify people through shared experience, specific responsibilities that allow them to achieve unique respect and offer it in kind to others, a genuinely meritocratic system that values contribution more than "seniority," and finally, some high-stakes environments or challenges that force people to work together under pressure.

LESSON

HOW TO PARENT AS A TEAM

1. Don't talk trash about your wife to your kids.

2. Don't embarrass her in front of the kids.

3. Take your wife's side in front of the kids, and if there is an issue, you tell her when you're both away from the kids.

Overall, my wife and I have found raising teenagers pretty easy. Our kids have had their moments, but they haven't been rebellious or disrespectful. Well . . . they haven't made a habit of it.

But one time, my oldest daughter was butting heads with my wife. This daughter was about thirteen, and while she and Tina have a great relationship, there are times when moms and their daughters start talking around one another in a way that someone from the outside can usually pick up on pretty quick, but which the people involved can't.

The teenage years can exacerbate this, as your kids are starting to develop their own opinions. Prescription begins to give way to explanation. It's a natural and necessary process, but the reason teenage years can be difficult is because boundaries are shifting at the same time that hormones are screaming and capabilities are increasing. It's a combustible cocktail.

In this particular moment, my daughter didn't feel like she was being heard, and my wife felt like she was being disrespected. As soon as disrespect enters the scene, parents feel the need to reassert authority. Because they do. Even if your child has a point, once disrespect is accepted, it transfers into other areas. It doesn't mean that you can't go back later and rehash the conversation or even apologize for not fully understanding the context. (I've had to do that.) However, disrespect has to be shut down in the moment.

In this particular case, my wife was in the process of asserting authority when my daughter started to leave the room. As she rounded the corner, she didn't see me or realize that I had a clear line of sight to the disrespectful face she was shooting my wife.

My daughter almost bumped into me and was visibly startled both by the encounter and by the knowledge that her little act of defiance might not have been as secret as she assumed. She stopped, eyes wide, almost certainly wondering if I had seen her.

I looked at her and very calmly but sternly said: "Don't ever treat my wife like that again."

"Yes, Daddy."

"Okay."

The distinction here is important.

Not "your mother," not "Mommy," but "my wife."

I've told this story before, and there are always people in the comments section with their opinions on whether this is a positive tactic. Some say it seems like bullying. Someone always objects: What about when the parent is wrong or abusive? Can I just say that I understand that there are always exceptions, but for the love of God, can we appreciate a perspective given in good faith without insisting that every exception to the rule be caveated before a point can be made? If your wife is a serial cheater or you are a degenerate gambler who has ruined your family's future, you should be solving those problems in your life before you start with any of the issues in this book.

There is a reason I did it this way. It wasn't only to have my wife's back: It was to create an expectation in my daughter that one day, when she inevitably has issues with her children, her husband should defend her!

I have a great relationship with my kids. That's partly because they grew up in an environment where they knew Mom and Dad were a team who supported one another. This meant the children never had to worry about divorce or instability in the house. Mom and Dad were good, and that made them safe.

> There will be times when you are wrong, or your wife is, and you may need to take each other aside and point that out, but you need to be a united front. Not just to your kids, but to your wife. Kids will pick up whenever Dad or Mom can be manipulated against the other. If you allow this to happen, you teach them to do it and, worse, expect it in their own marriages and families one day. In an otherwise healthy marriage and family life, Mom and Dad having each other's back is good for everyone.

LESSON 23

HOW TO GROW INTO A MAN OF GOD

I grew up in a Christian home, and it always made sense to me on some level. I can't remember a time when I didn't consider myself a Christian. But when I went into active duty at eighteen, you probably would have never guessed that I was a Christian or that it played much of a role in my life. I didn't regularly attend church, and my language took on the same flavor as just about everyone else. Other than saying I was a Christian, there wasn't much to go on.

This continued after I got married and even after we started having kids. Again, it wasn't that I didn't care or that I didn't believe; it just wasn't prevalent in my life the way it should have been. A few things changed that, or more specifically, three men I met during my time in Army Special Forces helped change that.

The first was my neighbor Anthony Brown. Anthony was as good a neighbor as you could ask for and definitely a man's man. A husband, father, veteran, electrician, reservist, and a no-nonsense kind of guy who you just knew had your back. Anthony was a little bit older than me, but not by much. Anthony and his wife, Janell, were our first very close friends that we had in our time in the military who weren't on active duty themselves. We would hang out, play games, raise our kids together, cook out, and talk about Christianity.

I remember one time Anthony telling me in the very matter-of-fact way he said just about everything, "Hey brother, don't know if you are the going-to-church type, but I am. And not pushing, but we are going to church on Sunday. If you ever want to go with us, you are more than welcome." That was it. No guilt, no why aren't you going, no sense of moral superiority about it, and no condemnation when we didn't go.

It wasn't long after that that Tina and I were discussing going to church, and my three-year-old at the time asked, "What's church?" That's what made me feel guilty, and appropriately so. We decided to go with Anthony, Janell, and their kids to church.

I know there are going to be some people who say things like "I don't need church." Or "My church is the outdoors." Or whatever else.

Look, just like Anthony, I'm not going to be pushy or condescending, but if you're a Christian, then please understand that your Bible tells you that you do need dedicated time with other believers for prayer, accountability, edification, and service. So, please understand that this isn't just "some opinion" or an attempt to get you somewhere to tithe. The "Church" is the body of believers, and while you may not need to attend a particular service at a particular building, you do need fellowship with other believers. If you don't like that, take it up with God, not me.

Okay, back to the story.

We started regularly going to church with the Browns, and even started serving in the church, which I came to realize was an important part of one's faith. Too often, we treat church as if it were a purely consumer-based environment where everyone should just be happy you showed up. Reality is that the church is supposed to be both a give and a take. Service with a group of believers is as necessary as attendance.

Church is like the gym. It's good to think about it. It's useful to see how others do it. But until you get in there and start lifting yourself, it's not going to be as fun, and it's not going to make you stronger.

I am incredibly grateful to Anthony for inviting us. I'm also grateful that he was the sort of man who could invite me to church that I would actually listen to. Anthony wasn't the first man to personally invite me to church since I went into the military. But he was one of the first whom I truly respected as being a "real man." Anthony was tough, no-nonsense, dependable, honest, and competent. He would set down anything he was doing in a heartbeat to help a friend, and I never had any doubt that he would have my back in a fight. Now you may ask why that matters. Well, to most men it does. To someone who was serving as a Green Beret in wartime, it really did. Whether you were willing to have my back and then capable of doing something in a fight was one of the ways we judged each other in the military. Anthony could and would, and it was because Anthony was all of those things that when he invited me to church, I listened.

I will forever be grateful to him for that.

The next guy who helped me discover an aspect of my faith that I had been missing is someone whose name I regret not remembering. He was National Guard Special Forces, and the only reason we even met was because we were attending the Special Forces Intelligence Sergeants Course at Fort Bragg, North Carolina.

He was very intelligent, articulate, and not afraid to get into an intellectual scrap about his faith, including with instructors. He was never brash or overly hostile about it, just bold and unapologetic, and he was good at his job.

I want to emphasize this for a moment. I was a kid in the '80s and '90s. This was when Christian movies and Christian music were trying to break into the regular scene. And let's face it—it was rough at times. There were many situations where we would listen to or watch

Christian entertainment because it was Christian, not because it was "good." It may have been wholesome, and I give credit where credit is due to people trying to engage in the difficult world of arts and entertainment, especially with a fraction of the budgets that their secular counterparts had, but while the mission was noble and the effort was sincere, the quality was sometimes lacking. I had kind of gotten used to this idea that I was supposed to ignore the quality of something if it was "Christian" and the professional competency of someone if they were "Christian." But I was in the military. Professional competency was pretty important, and oftentimes it was the very uncouth, hard-assed NCO who drank and cursed enough to make a longshoreman blush who was the guy you emulated. But this guy was different.

His Christianity wasn't an excuse for lack of performance or lack of boldness. His Christianity seemed to be the cause of his boldness and high performance. There is peer pressure everywhere to include Special Forces, and nothing would have been easier than for this guy to just go with the flow or keep his head down. It's not like people trashed you for your faith in the military; just don't mention it all the time, and you'll be fine. This guy would get up on Friday afternoon and say to a classroom of fifty-one Green Berets, "Hey, I just want everyone to know we have church and BBQ on Sunday. If you want to go, let me know, plenty of room for everyone."

Again, not judgmental, not condescending, just matter-of-fact.

His competence extended from his job to his defense of the faith. This guy could debate. He could take on multiple students and an instructor all at once and come out on top. It's not like he went looking for the fight, but when the topic came up, he knew his stuff and could argue logically, historically, and empirically. It got to the point where everyone, even those who disagreed with him, didn't mock him, because they knew that while he wasn't trying to make them look stupid, stupid is exactly how they would look if they tried any of their tired Sky Daddy arguments against him.

On more than one occasion, we ended up on the same side of

some of these debates, and I will never forget him telling me, "You should look into Christian apologetics." I had no idea what that was, so he explained that apologetics was the intellectual defense of the faith. *Apologetics* comes from the Greek *apologia*, which means to speak in one's defense. That got me started down a path of listening and watching a number of Christian apologists, from William Lane Craig and Greg Bahnsen to Thomas Aquinas and many, many others over the years.

It was as if an entirely new aspect of my faith had just been discovered. Many of the churches I had grown up in might have been described as "charismatic." While there is certainly nothing wrong with wanting to appeal to a wide audience or to use language that can be understood by people not immersed in Scripture or Christian culture, there is something wrong with watered-down faith or treating your relationship with Christ like it's a kind of "self-help" approach to life. I realized that while my mother had certainly tried to inject a more intellectual side of the faith, she hadn't gotten a lot of help from youth leaders who, at the time, treated Christianity like it was chasing a high. Youth group, in some cases, seemed more about creating a vibe than about actual teaching. Christianity seemed overly emotional.

This fellow Green Beret helped me find the intellectual side of my faith. I can't emphasize how important this is.

Christians used to be known as the world's greatest scientists, mathematicians, physicists, teachers, and biologists, all in the name of better understanding God's creation. Then, within a relatively short period of time, the idea that God and science were somehow at war with one another was widely promulgated by secularists and atheists, and unfortunately, many Christians seemed to be fine with that. Well, I wasn't. I didn't want to believe in Christianity because it made me "feel good." I wanted to believe it if it was true. Studying the apologists helped me recapture the intellectual component of my faith and to realize that God commands us to do this. God is not afraid of Richard Dawkins. Because Christianity is not just a "religious tradition" or a "noble myth" but instead a relationship with God, the intellectual MUST be a component. Mark 12:30 says as much when we are commanded, "You shall love the Lord your God with all your heart, and with all of your soul and with all of your mind and with all of your strength."

A genuine, meaningful relationship includes the mind. Watching this man, who was competent and capable in his duties as a soldier, provide a bold and intellectually rigorous defense of his faith was a life-changing experience. Christianity is not meant to be just "deeply personal" and therefore relegated out of the public square. It is a foundational worldview based on a relationship with God, and because it is true, it deserves to be effectively defended by those who claim it.

The final gentleman I will speak of is Ryan Nenaber. Ryan was my detachment commander of ODA 1333 from 2006 to 2008 and one of the finest officers I ever worked for. Let me start by saying that Ryan and I are almost nothing alike in terms of personality. I am extroverted, often loud, and outgoing. Ryan was much more reserved, quiet, and contemplative.

Ryan was not a big guy, didn't really drink, never cussed, and was the furthest thing away from Patton you could imagine, except in one regard. He was not the least bit fazed when it came to danger or making a decision. He was always ready to listen to an opposing perspective or opinion from one of his NCOs, but when he made a decision, it was respected.

Ryan was another person who was bold in his faith, but in a different way. He was happy to talk about it if you were interested, but not pushy at all. His argument for what he believed was in the way he lived. I don't recall Ryan ever making a decision or engaging in an act I wouldn't refer to as honorable.

He was also a competent leader of men. Even men who were very different from him. I served with a lot of great guys throughout my time in the military. But most of them, especially in Special Forces, were what you might refer to as alpha males. Ryan made me realize that there is a difference between being an alpha and just being an ass.

Ryan was confident, competent, and above all, honorable. He demonstrated a kind of quiet leadership that was not flashy or arrogant but always trustworthy. We also found out later that he was an excellent boxer at West Point who used to play "What a Wonderful World" as his walkout music right before he showed someone what the mat tasted like.

So, what did all these men have in common?

Honor, competence, capability, self-sacrifice, intelligence, boldness, and courage.

In short, they behaved the way a man should. They represented what it meant to be a Man of God. I wanted to be like that. I still do.

LESSON 24

HOW TO BE DANGEROUS *FOR* YOUR FAMILY

1. Stay in shape.

2. Know how to fight.

3. Know when it is appropriate to fight.

4. If you do have to fight: win.

There is a side of me that has been seen by relatively few people. Most of them are in Iraq. The closest my wife ever saw of it was a message I left for someone who had threatened her. She remarked that something had changed in my voice and face that she had never seen before. It didn't scare her, per se, because she knew it was on her behalf, but for a brief moment, she caught a glimpse of what other people had seen in combat.

I remember seeing that same thing from my father once.

I was about fifteen, and he asked me if I wanted to go to work with him. Since he was an LAPD homicide detective, my answer was a very enthusiastic yes. We got up early in the morning and made the somewhat long drive from Chino to Los Angeles, and specifically South Bureau Homicide, where my dad met up with his partner, Rob. It was going to be a slow day, as evidenced by the fact that I was allowed to be there, so my dad, realizing that I didn't have much to do, asked me if I wanted to look through a crime scene book of cold cases. I don't know what father-son time looked like for most kids, but it was pretty epic for me!

At some point, my dad needed coffee, and I needed to use the restroom, so he escorted me back to the break room area. As we were walking back, my dad had a file in one hand and a pot of coffee in the other. In the hallway was a guy, probably late teens / early twenties, covered in tattoos, handcuffed to the bench. I quietly asked my dad what the tattoos meant, and he stopped and started to point them out when the guy lifted his head up to look at me, and my father's tone changed instantly as he told him sharply, "Keep your head down." I remember in that moment just wanting to get back to the desk, but my father proceeded to calmly explain in his previous tone the significance of the various tattoos and what they told him about the guy's gang affiliation, and so on. Then we walked back to the desk as if nothing of much consequence had happened.

It sounds relatively insignificant. A two-second exchange between my dad and a guy cuffed to a bench, and another thirty seconds to provide some brief insight into the world of gang tattoos. Nothing you would think would be formative. And yet here I am thirty years later, a combat veteran and former Special Forces operator, telling you about it.

I always knew that, of course, there must be another side to my father. He had worked in one of the most dangerous divisions in LA for eleven years and was now tracking down murderers. But it's one thing to intuitively assume something. It's another thing to get the faintest glimpse of it and feel the whole room shift, if only for a moment, and in that act recognize that for some people that was the only side of my father they knew. Not the witty guy who took you to Dodgers games and played catch with you, even when he was obviously tired. But a dangerous man. A man who could invoke fear in someone instantly by a change in tone, which signified both his willingness and ability to go from a casual explanation to overwhelming violence as the situation required.

None of what happened that day scared me. It made me feel protected by my father. I wanted to provide that for my wife and children one day. To be able to change a tone and have it be instantly understood as what was possible. To be not only willing but capable of judicious violence when needed. To be dangerous for my family, but never to them.

Because let's face it, there are husbands and fathers out there who don't know how to develop the skills necessary to be dangerous without making their family feel unsafe. The bottom line is it's not good enough to just be strong and capable in a fight. You must develop the emotional maturity to complement the physical prowess.

I have had my share of moments where my frustration got the best of me, and while I would never hurt my wife or kids, there were definitely times when I could have handled my stress a lot better. Remember that your family knowing you're powerful can build trust and security or fear and anxiety. Protecting is about achieving not just their physical safety but their emotional safety as well.

Let's be honest, it isn't always easy to navigate the world between "protector" and loving husband or gentle father.

First of all, if you are struggling with something, make sure you have another male friend you respect as a man whom you can talk to and who can hold you accountable. Sometimes we just need to talk to another guy, and that is fine; just make sure he is someone who shares your principles and wants you to be successful. That way, he can bring support or correction when needed, and you can be confident that either way, it's from a place of genuine concern for you and your family.

Another source of frustration when it comes to protecting your family stems from their not understanding or appreciating why you do the things you do.

One thing I did to make my family aware of the danger in the world, without making them afraid of it, was to discuss with them why Dad did the things he did. Maybe it was simple, like walking on the street side when we were all on the sidewalk, or sitting where I could see the door at a restaurant. Maybe it was discussing what I expected them to do in a fire, or if we were at a busy amusement park. Discussing these things did two things right off the bat. It made them feel like they were a part of the plan and let them know that Dad was vigilant.

Seeing something on a show or noticing something in public, I might stop and ask my kids what they thought or how they might handle a situation. This helped foster awareness and empowerment rather than fear. This process also ensured that whenever we were in a situation and I needed them to move and move quickly without questioning, they did, because they had already been prepared.

The bottom line is that this is not negotiable. Men protect. So, develop the proper physical and emotional skills to do it correctly, and you will be shocked to see the kind of impact it has on your family. Your wife and kids will feel safe. Your kids will also think it's awesome (especially your son), and your wife will think it's hot.

LESSON

HOW TO COOK FOR OTHERS

1. Start with something you like. Preferably something nobody else in the house already makes.

2. Find a recipe online and then skip all the stuff about how their "grandmama from Tuscany fell in love with a GI, when all of a sudden . . ." Seriously, you'll just be looking for ingredients, and all of a sudden, you're in the middle of a Hallmark movie. Just skip to the recipe.

3. Don't screw with the recipe the first time out. Just follow the instructions even when they seem weird. YouTube is your friend if you don't understand what the instructions mean.

4. Don't just grill. Learn how to do other stuff. It's a good skill to have, and your wife will think it's cute when you try and hot when you get it right.

A man should know how to cook. In my home, there is zero doubt that my wife is the cook. She is fantastic at it. It has gotten to the point that eating out just feels like a complete letdown, because we all know that Mommy can do it better at home.

Still, your wife and your children will really appreciate it if Dad can cook more than just steak and eggs.

I could always do some very basic grilling, but I actually didn't start learning how to cook more complex dishes until COVID. This is something I regret. I learned that I enjoy it. In fact, over time, while my wife remains the all-time undisputed champion of our kitchen, a few dishes have become my domain.

How do you get started when your wife cooks everything better than you? You start with things she may like but doesn't enjoy cooking, or something that you want to try but doesn't typically get cooked.

For me, it was a couple of different things: Fried chicken. Spaghetti and sauce. General Tso's chicken. Prime rib. None of these is prohibitively difficult. The General Tso is a little more tricky, but not too terrible.

For the spaghetti, that was pretty easy: I just followed Grandma's recipe. Over time, I tweaked things here and there to my taste and the taste of my family.

The General Tso I've done only a few times, in part because I get too frustrated with it, and since it was never really a family favorite, I didn't have to improve.

Prime rib, I really only make for Christmas dinner as a way to give my wife time off and to perfect my approach.

But the fried chicken, especially my chicken nuggets, I take pride in that. Again, not terribly difficult, but I have learned how to make them to my family's taste and even a gluten-free version that passes muster. When my kids find out I'm making chicken nuggets, the friends come over, my son-in-law comes over, and honestly, it's become fun to know that there is a dish that can bring people over to eat and chat together.

We made cooking a part of our kids' homeschool curriculum. One year for our anniversary during COVID, we had all gotten into watching baking competitions, and so our kids' present was for each of them to make an anniversary-themed cake for us. They all did a great job, and the youngest was thrilled to win best in show.

Since then, they have all started to cook more, in part because some days we intentionally tell them it's their turn, and other days we just forget and then pretend that we planned to make it an on-the-spot assignment.

Our oldest daughter became the first to master sourdough bread, which in our home is a form of currency. Our son specializes in cheesecakes, nachos, and pretty elaborate ramen. I don't mean the stuff you get in the package at Walmart. I mean, they go to the H-Mart Asian grocery in Northern Virginia and then spend four hours making RAMEN ramen. Our youngest daughter makes some incredible taco and Italian dishes and is also a baker, usually of all the things we are desperately trying to avoid.

All of them enjoy being known for certain things and appreciate it when we are all excited that they made "their thing"!

So how do you start?

I would recommend trying some different recipes based on your tastes. If you actually like what you're cooking, you will want to try it more. Different types of cooking have varying difficulty levels, and some are far more forgiving than others.

For instance, baking can be pretty straightforward if it's a pie, but if you're doing something like homemade sourdough, expect a lot of trial and error.

Grilling can be easy, especially if you're going for something simple like a dry rub. Smoking meat is a lot more in-depth. However, there are smokers now that make it significantly easier than it used to be.

Pick some kind of protein you want to try. Beef, pork, and poultry are obviously the most common. Salmon can be pretty easy. Lamb is a little more challenging. If I were starting all over again, I would probably just begin with making a really good New York strip or filet. Get my seasonings down and monitor grilling time with a thermometer. If I didn't have a grill, I would go cast iron, with seasonings and lots of butter.

Side dish, I'd go with asparagus, or maybe baked brussels sprouts. You may be thinking "brussels sprouts?? The vegetable everyone makes fun of?" Yes. Boiled or steamed brussels sprouts are not great. Better than when we were kids (thanks to the miracle of agricultural science), but not great. Properly seasoned and grilled or roasted, they are incredible.

For a dessert, cheesecakes are not terribly difficult. I like German shortbread cookies with walnuts, so I got good at that, and now everyone loves it when I make them.

Now, for the guy who has never cooked before, let me share something with you about looking up recipes online. Every time you look one up, it's going to show you something incredible, and then go into a twelve-paragraph story about "the origin of garlic and how Grandma used to make this dish every . . ." but there will almost always be a "skip to recipe" button you can push.

If you don't have a roll of parchment paper and a cheap digital cooking thermometer, get them.

When you first start, follow the recipe with respect to ingredients, but remember that stoves and grills can cook differently, and there will often be a difference between the temperature your stove indicates and the actual temperature. Get yourself a decent external thermometer. Ideally, one that can connect to your phone and COOK TO TEMP when it comes to things like meat.

Once you have successfully pulled off a decent meal based on the recipe, start cooking to taste and temp.

If it comes out bland, it usually needs more salt, fat, acid, or all three. Butter is usually the best fat, and lemon juice is the best acid. When you can't figure out why your food isn't as good as your favorite restaurant's, the answer is almost always that they used twice as much salt and three times as much butter as you did.

Oh, and YouTube can be your friend when you don't understand the written directions.

I'm not saying you have to be a full-blown chef, but the ladies do love it when you can put something together that doesn't come from a box with the word *helper* on the side. Being able to cook well pays a number of dividends because it also shows attention to detail, competence, the ability to follow instructions, innovation, and when you are making something she particularly likes, thoughtfulness and affection.

One other thing . . . learn to be a "clean cook." If every time you cook, you blow up the kitchen, you might be creating more work than your food is worth. Ask me how I know . . . I got better.

LESSON 26

HOW TO MAKE YOUR DAUGHTER FEEL LOVED

1. Tell her you love her.

2. Show you love her with quality time, discussion, daddy-daughter dates, and so forth.

3. Tell her the truth.

4. Be there when she needs to talk and listen, especially being willing to hear the truth from her, even when you don't like it.

5. Treat her mother well.

You want to know the most annoying thing about telling fathers that they need to tell their daughters they love them? The almost instant response you will get from people on the internet who have never seen anything else you have ever written or spoken about on the subject obnoxiously reminding you: "That's not enough, you have to show them you love them! Actions speak louder than words."

No kidding?

Thanks, internet rando! I really appreciate that amazing follow-up to a thirty-six-second clip of a two-hour podcast you just commented on! So, before I get started on the importance of fathers TELLING their daughters they love them, let me assure everyone that I, too, believe that hollow, verbal expressions of love devoid of any of the necessary corresponding actions and sacrifice are not a sufficient manifestation of this vital entity we call "love."

Can we move on now?

Fathers. Tell your daughters you love them.

The reason I emphasize this point is that many of the things fathers do, such as protecting and providing for their children, are legitimate and necessary manifestations of love, but your kids need to make that connection, and the earlier they do, the better.

Some of this advice came from a guy I served in the Army with who was one of the biggest man-whores I knew. This guy had women throwing themselves at him with minimal effort. He wasn't tall or rich. He was a reasonably good-looking guy, but not gorgeous or anything, and yet, beautiful women couldn't seem to say no. So, I asked him, "How do I protect my daughter from a guy like you?" With almost no hesitation, he said, "Tell your daughter you love her. Because if you don't, someone who doesn't will, and she will believe them."

He was very matter-of-fact about it. And as a father, I was grateful for the information. And, while it seems obvious, there is actually a lot packed into that simple statement.

This may come as a shock to modern leftism, but boys and girls are different, and while they need a lot of the same things, there are different reasons and ways to deliver those needed things optimally for them.

There were three basic things that I did to try to reinforce to my daughters that I loved them, as well as help them to distinguish between genuine love and the fake kind.

1. **I verbally told my daughters I loved them.** This was backed up by actions. When they were little, I had the little tea parties, chased them around the house as the tickle monster, and made silly jokes they thought were hilarious at the time. As time went on, I took an interest in their interests, discussed things with them, and focused on listening to them as they explained their social dynamics and issues they were facing. The end result was that they didn't associate "love" just with me providing and protecting them, but with me taking a genuine interest in who they were as a person, intellectually, emotionally, and spiritually. I could have done those things without saying I love you, but then the connection might not have been there. Saying "I love you" reinforces to them that this is what someone who loves you does. So, if you hear "I love you" but only when someone wants something from you, you clearly understand that it is counterfeit. Not because you studied the counterfeit, but because you have spent so much time with the genuine article that everything else is easily recognized as the fake it is.

2. **I told them the truth.** This is more important than I can adequately express here. Let me explain this carefully. That did not mean that I was harsh or cruel. If I ever had to tell my daughters something I knew they didn't want to hear, I was very careful in how I worded it so that they knew I was on their side. I didn't relish telling them hard truths; I was both protecting and preparing them. Oftentimes, I would ask them questions about an issue or a problem to let them come to their own conclusions.

As long as they were respectful in the process, I would listen to opposition and challenges to my reasoning and understanding. As a result, a couple of things developed:

They knew they could talk to Dad about things that were bothering or frustrating them. If they needed to vent, I would listen; if they needed to work it out intellectually, I would engage with them. But there was a rule. Truth was the goal.

They learned how to engage their feelings but not be led by them. Feelings are an invitation to thought. Feelings were valid, but they didn't trump reality. The goal was to identify what the truth was and to base one's feelings on that.

Telling my daughters the truth with love meant they could trust that if they asked me a question or wanted to discuss a problem, they were doing it with someone who was absolutely dedicated to their success. Never having to question my love or loyalty meant that we could discuss the hard questions in a safe place.

3. **They could tell me the truth.** This builds off the previous paragraph. It is a great thing for your daughters to want you to be proud of them. It's perfectly appropriate for them not to want to disappoint Dad. But I would argue that the real indicator of a strong relationship is not just a daughter who makes good decisions but a daughter who is willing to come to you when she has made a bad one, or . . . when you have. How you behave when your daughter tells you a hard truth, in the form of either a confession or a correction, will tell her a lot about how safe a place you are to confide in. Set the pattern early by rewarding her when she tells you the truth and by showing

her that ultimately, you will always be there to pick her up when she falls. When you've proved that, you will find that you become one of the first people your daughter talks things through with instead of hiding things from.

I found that what this achieved was daughters who knew what genuine love should look like and were confident that Dad wouldn't steer them in the wrong direction. With one daughter married and the other now sixteen, I can tell you this has worked for me, but more important, it has worked for them.

Plus, I taught them how to shoot. Just in case.

LESSON 27

HOW TO WIN AN ARGUMENT

There is no shortage of bad arguments made on the regular. The fastest way to defeat them is usually just to ask people to explain themselves. Most people don't have any of the facts, and they haven't gone through the argument. They just know they're right based on vibes.

Sometimes we know there is something wrong with the argument, but we're not sure how to articulate it. This chapter is going to equip you with what you need to not only spot fallacies but be able to call them out.

Fallacies fall into one of two broad categories. Formal and informal. Just like how arguments are graded on both structure and soundness or whether they are cogent, fallacies are also "structure-based" or "content-based."

All formal fallacies are a form of "non sequitur," which is fancy Latin talk for "does not follow." That's just another way to say that the inference or conclusion doesn't follow from the premise.

EXAMPLE:

1. Premise 1: All cats are evil.

2. Premise 2: The word *evil* starts with the letter E.

3. Inference: The word *cat* starts with the letter E.

But here is the crazy part. A non sequitur can still be true.

EXAMPLE:

1. Premise 1: All cats are evil.

2. Premise 2: The word *evil* starts with the letter E.

3. Inference: Cats are mammals.

Nothing about that statement makes sense, yet it's still true. The problem is not with the truth of the conclusion, but how you got there.

Sometimes these can be the most frustrating of arguments to contend with, because it is a diagnosis problem. People get to the correct conclusion purely by accident, which leads them to believe that they are using sound reasoning when in reality they got lucky.

If you want to learn more about formal fallacies, there is a seemingly never-ending supply of literature and videos online. It's a good thing to understand, but I'm going to spend the majority of this chapter discussing informal fallacies.

Informal fallacies are arguments that are unsound or lack strong premises. Again, a seemingly never-ending list, but we will cover some of the most obvious and frequently used.

1. **Ad hominem:** This is Latin for "attacking the man." This is when someone attempts to negate your argument not by addressing your premises, evidence, or conclusions but by diminishing your standing to even give such an argument.

Example: "You talk about the dangers of drunk driving, but you're a drunk!"

Flaw: Not only can you be a drunk and correct about the dangers of drunk driving, you can be driving drunk while discussing the dangers of drunk driving and still be correct. (Never do this, BTW.) Your actions or history, in this case, have no bearing on whether your argument is correct. Arguments should be judged based on the premises and conclusion, not the character or circumstances of the person making the argument.

Rebuttal: "How does your attacking me personally invalidate my statement?"

But on the other hand, you shouldn't dismiss an argument outright because of the character of the person making the argument. It's important to remember that people do not like hypocrisy, and saying one thing and doing another, or disregarding your own advice, can have negative consequences with respect to how people view your sincerity.

2. **Straw Man:** This is when someone misrepresents an argument by making a weaker version of it and then acting as if that were the actual argument.

   Example: "You think keeping your guns is more important than keeping children safe!"

   Flaw: Assuming that the primary threat is the instrument itself rather than the person using it.

   Rebuttal: "When a school shooting takes place, is everyone's first instinct to call people with guns to come and stop it?"

3. **Red Herring:** This is when someone brings up an unrelated fact or topic. Usually, one that appears related in some way, but either is not or is so far removed from the discussion as to be a deliberate distraction.

   Example: "You say you oppose abortion, but how many kids have you adopted?"

   Flaw: While something like adoption is tangentially related to the topic, it is not a necessary precondition for one to have a position on the destruction of innocent human life in the womb.

   Rebuttal: "Would someone have had to personally hide a Jewish person from the Nazis to believe that the Holocaust was wrong?"

   But on the other hand, not all tangential arguments are completely invalid. While it may be perfectly appropriate to call out a red herring when you see it, make sure that it is, in fact, a red herring, and not just a different but relevant point to the topic of discussion.

4. **Hasty Generalization:** This is when someone draws sweeping conclusions based on very limited evidence or experience.

   Example: "I had a very bad experience with a toxic boyfriend. You just can't trust men."

   Flaw: There are quite literally billions of men in the world. Having a bad experience with one does not translate to general toxicity in all of them.

Rebuttal: "Should we judge every man on the planet by the experiences you had with one? Would you want every woman to be judged that way?"

5. **Appeal to Authority:** This is when a person's opinion is accepted as true exclusively based on their credentials as an "expert."

    Example: "A professor at Harvard says tariffs cause inflation."

    Flaw: Experts SHOULD have a higher probability of being correct on a particular topic, but their credentials alone do not determine whether they are correct. Their arguments need to be supported by proof.

    Rebuttal: "I am more than happy to listen to an expert make an argument, but credentials don't equal truth. I can find an economist who says they don't. I'd rather compare their arguments than their résumés."

6. **False Dilemma:** Presenting limited options as if they were the only ones available in order to limit the number of acceptable answers.

    Example: "You're either with us, or you're with the terrorists."

    Flaw: The implication in this statement is that if you do not support certain specific actions taken to combat terrorism, you must be for the terrorists. In reality, you can oppose terrorism and someone's approach to dealing with the problem.

Rebuttal: "Are you really suggesting that the only options I have are invade Iraq or donate to Bin Laden? What if I said you are either with ME or you're with the terrorists? Can't I apply the same logic to you?"

But on the other hand, sometimes there may technically be other options; however, if only two are practical, then something can be "technically" a false dilemma but "practically" genuine. A good example of this might be an election, where there are several candidates, but only a few who have any shot of winning.

7. **Appeal to Pity/Emotion:** Presenting a case based on a purely emotional appeal rather than sufficient facts and evidence.

   Example: "You can't cut that government program because it will cause the people working for it to lose their jobs. In fact, I have this one very tragic example involving a family with medical bills."

   Flaw: Our attention is being directed away from the question of whether the government should be doing something to what the effects will be on the person performing the task.

   Rebuttal: "Every change in a policy is going to create winners and losers. Forcing other people with jobs to contribute to the creation of a job that is not needed is neither sound nor compassionate."

   But on the other hand, in the real world, where a lot of decisions are made on emotional appeals, it's important to understand why. Emotional appeals work because, ultimately, we want to at least be seen as caring people. When making an argument, use emotional appeals. Just make sure that your emotional appeal is backed up by facts and logic. That's how you get the best of both worlds.

8. **Genetic Fallacy:** This is when someone automatically discounts or believes a piece of information based on the source.

    Example: "I don't believe ANYTHING Fox News puts out."

    Flaw: While it may be perfectly appropriate to be skeptical of certain sources, based on their history or reputation, that does not determine whether something is true.

    Rebuttal: "I think I understand why you are skeptical of that source, but why do you believe this specific claim is false?"

    But on the other hand, because all of us rely on incomplete information to make decisions, especially about events and topics we are not personally involved in, we necessarily utilize "heuristics." These are mental shortcuts that allow us to make decisions based on information from trusted sources. So, while it's true that the genetic fallacy is in fact a fallacy, legitimate trust issues are good reasons to ignore a particular source, especially if other, more trusted ones are present.

9. **Causation Versus Correlation Fallacy:** This is when an outcome coincides with other factors; therefore, it is assumed that those factors caused the outcome.

    Example: "We had record job growth under Biden. Bidenomics works!"

Flaw: Job growth, like so many things, is not necessarily a direct result of a particular president's policies. A more extreme example is "Every time the sun comes up, my rooster crows, therefore my rooster crowing is responsible for the sunrise."

Rebuttal: "Can you please tell me what specific policies within Bidenomics you believe directly contributed to job growth?"

But on the other hand, correlation might not be causation, and a lack of correlation certainly isn't causation. By that I mean, when debating this with someone, you might want to have an alternative explanation ready for why you think something actually happened.

Finally, please remember that not every argument is worth your time. If someone is willing to argue in good faith, I am here for it. But once it has been demonstrated that there is no objective standard they are willing to stick to, it may be time to simply thank them for the conversation and move on. Jesus talks about "throwing pearls before swine." It's not meant to be an insult, suggesting that someone is a pig, but a reminder that if someone displays zero interest in a good-faith discussion, they may be distracting you from someone who could benefit from one.

LESSON 28

HOW TO LEARN FROM YOUR PARENTS

1. Appreciate what they had to go through before you came along.

2. Appreciate what they did right.

3. Appreciate that no one gets parenting completely right.

This is, of course, assuming your parents weren't complete deadbeats.

If they were the sort of people who physically and sexually abused you, feel free not to give them a break. But for most of us, your parents are probably not as bad as your woke therapist has been trained to tell you they are. Nothing makes this more apparent than when you have your own kids and realize that some of the mistakes your parents may have made are suddenly pretty understandable.

I remember the first time someone told me I was from a "broken home." The statement was technically true, but I couldn't help feeling that it was something of an accusation. A revelation about my circumstances that I had always been somewhat aware of, but never quite accepted.

My parents separated shortly after my younger brother was born. I was about four when they divorced. To top it off, at the time this well-intentioned individual was informing me of the "brokenness" of my home, my mother was separated from my stepdad, so let's be honest, it was kind of difficult to argue with his description.

The thing is, I didn't feel that way about my family. Which is to say I didn't feel "broken." That was probably due largely to the fact that my mother and my father were both involved in my life, and they didn't attempt to use me or my brother as pawns.

Sure, there were disagreements and conflict, but I was never subjected to the experience where the kids become the strategic terrain in a war between Dad and Mom. So let me acknowledge up front that although I came from a divorce, it was definitely on the "softer" side of it, because my parents tried to handle it with a degree of respect and maturity toward one another. And I am forever grateful for that!

In addition to my experience, I have seen other parents who have come through the wringer. Friends who had to fight through poverty, neglect, and physical, mental, and sometimes even sexual abuse. They come out on the other side of their childhood, get married, raise kids, and quite incredibly break the cycle that tormented their youth. And their thanks for that effort is to have one or more of their children focus exclusively on how Mom would get "easily frustrated" or "Dad yelled sometimes" as if this were some kind of soul-crushing trauma they endured and for which their parents need to be forever apologetic.

Can I just say with all sincerity: Grow the hell up.

Nobody's parents are perfect; all of them have their own baggage, some of them overcame incredible challenges to make life better than they had it, and for the love of God, if that was your parents' situation, show them a little bit of grace. I'm not telling you to forget significant problems or to ignore the deficiencies in their parenting that you may want to correct when your time comes. Still, context and gratitude go a long way in shaping a healthy perspective on life.

So, if your parents were horribly abusive individuals, I'm not telling you to give them a break. Just please differentiate between "horribly abusive" and "just human." Because it seems like we have a never-ending stream of dorm room psychologists who have a hard time distinguishing between the two, with the end result being horribly self-centered "adult" children, incapable of understanding what their own parents may have had to go through to make life significantly better for their kids.

LESSON 29

HOW TO VALUE MASCULINITY

1. No successful civilization in history has ever survived without it.

2. Families suffer from a lack of it.

3. Even feminists complain about a lack of it in the guys they date.

Over the past few decades, women in America have become less happy, according to polls. At the same time, men have been told that traditionally masculine traits are toxic.

Interesting, right? By "masculinity," I mean those traits generally associated with men. Physical strength, bravery, aggression, competitiveness, stoicism, a mechanical mind, and a desire to have more sex. When I speak of "toxicity," I mean something that poisons or negatively affects what it comes into contact with.

Can certain masculine traits be applied in a way that could be categorized as "toxic"? Sure. Then why is there such a problem with the term *toxic masculinity*? Haven't I just admitted toxic masculinity exists?

Before I answer someone who poses this question to me, I always ask them if there is such a thing as "toxic femininity." If they immediately shy away from the term, I know I am probably not having a good-faith discussion with them.

The real issue is that *toxic masculinity*, like many terms commonly used by the Left, expands and shrinks based on the audience.

When a critic of toxic masculinity is speaking to a room full of supporters, a whole host of masculine traits, from aggression to competitiveness, not to mention mannerisms associated with gentlemanliness, such as opening doors or giving up your seat on the subway, is proudly derided as "toxic" behavior, usually to applause.

But the moment the crowd is mixed, or more academic in nature, suddenly, toxic masculinity is reduced to its most sympathetic examples, and the speaker or questioner essentially dares you to reject the notion that men have never done horrible things. See how that works? We didn't discuss the motte-and-bailey fallacy in the last lesson, but this is it. State something controversial ("opening a door for someone is toxic"), and when challenged, pretend you were arguing something noncontroversial ("are you saying it's okay to treat women like a piece of meat?").

You can find feminists willing to continue this process until the definition expands to include just about anything required in the heat of the moment.

Are you arguing with a woman and attempting to clearly explain your position? That's "mansplaining," and that's toxic.

Are you not arguing with a woman because you decide to just give up? You're not properly engaging or hearing her, and that's toxic.

Did you open the door for a woman? That insinuates that you think she is incapable of opening it for herself. That's old-fashioned misogyny, and that's toxic.

Did you fail to open the door for a woman? That is rude and dismissive behavior, and that's toxic.

Toxic masculinity has become a colloquial catchall for anything a man does that might irritate a woman in the moment. It provides a moral justification for trashing men instead of attempting to understand their perspective.

Is there such a thing as "mansplaining"?

If by "mansplaining" you mean a man being condescending to a woman based on a sexist insistence that she couldn't possibly understand something, that would at least be a grievance I could understand. But would women like it if we called an overly emotional reaction to an event being "her-sterical"? Because we can all play this game if we would like to.

Or we can acknowledge some fairly easy-to-understand truths. Men and women are different. (Pause for reader gasps.)

There are various traits and characteristics that fall into broad categories of the masculine or the feminine because, on average, men and women tend to display different characteristics. Many of them are morally neutral outside a larger context. Male aggression can be used for positive ends or ill. Female empathy can be used to comfort a friend or manipulate them.

The goal should be to recognize the positive and negative manifestations of these traits, recognize that when we focus on the positive manifestations, not only are they a good in and of themselves, but they are often complementary. This is why children typically do so much better in a healthy household where there is both a mother and a father.

So maybe we should abandon what have become highly disingenuous terms like *toxic masculinity* and instead recognize that masculine and feminine traits are there for a reason and, when properly developed, applied, and appreciated, are good, necessary, and complementary.

Again, if women were actually happy with the sort of males who wholeheartedly accept these broad definitions of toxic masculinity and respond accordingly, they would probably date or even marry them. But they don't. Not even liberal women seem to like woke, feminist men very much.

In the future, feel free to respectfully say no to pink dress shirts, Hallmark movies, pedicures, Adele, earrings, gossip, HomeGoods, musicals, TikTok dances, texting your friends about your feelings, mimosas, or paying someone to change the windshield wipers on your car. Your female friends may say they value these things, but when they call you and ask for help, it won't be for any of these things. It will be because they need something heavy moved around.

LESSON 30

HOW TO CONDUCT BASIC FIRST AID

1. If possible, call or have someone call first responders. Don't assume someone else did it.

2. Assess the situation. Is the injured person out of danger? Giving really good CPR is not helpful if the car they are in is about to catch fire.

3. Assess consciousness, breathing, and bleeding. If they can talk, they can usually breath. Focus on breathing and bleeding, because it's super hard to live without air or blood.

4. Deal with bad arterial bleeds before breathing issues, because that will kill you faster than not having air. (In cases where severe trauma is not involved, breathing issues are more likely to be the greater threat.)

5. Once bleeding is stopped and breathing is steady, keep the injured person covered and speak with them until real help arrives.

Knowing what first aid is and how to properly apply it is essential. I remember when I first went into the military, we would do cross-training with our medics on how to assess the situation, apply bandages, and so on.

Back then, it was all about the ABCs: airway, breathing, and circulation (which was really about bleeding, but the "ABBs" doesn't sound as cool).

The idea was that when you came upon a casualty, you always did a quick top-to-bottom, front-to-back assessment to make sure you had properly identified all the most pressing issues. A lot of scenarios would be set up to grab your attention with something obvious and get you focused on that, while the poor sap bled out because of a wound somewhere else.

Later on in the military, everything became about stopping the bleeding, since it turns out that in combat, keeping the blood in the body and then getting follow-on care was the single best way to save someone's life.

Most basic first aid situations you are going to be in probably won't have the same conditions as combat, and so it's important to differentiate between combat first aid and more common everyday situations you may encounter. (Stopping the bleeding remains incredibly important, if that's the issue you encounter.)

So here are some basic things to keep in mind.

Assess the Situation: Depending on the circumstances, the first thing you may need to do is assess the situation. Jumping out of a car to help as soon as an accident happens right in front of you might be a noble instinct, but if it results in you getting hit as well, you just became part of the problem. Any sort of environment where you have the potential for more injuries to take place is a problem. Sometimes you have to secure the environment to some degree before you can begin rendering aid. Obviously, if a kid falls in the pool, you don't have to conduct a thorough analysis of the situation before acting, but preventing a three-car pileup from becoming a nine-car pileup is a good place to start.

Assess the Individual: The primary thing you are looking for here is responsiveness and whether they are still in danger. There are all kinds of questions on the best thing to do for a variety of injuries, but if they are face down in the pool or in a burning house or car, what they need just then is either to have the threat mitigated or to be moved away from it. This is especially important for triage situations where you may have several people injured. Get people out of danger, then move to the next steps. If you find yourself in a dangerous situation and you are not capable of removing them from it, calling for assistance is your next step. Again, don't let a desire to be brave push you to do something that will only cause you to be a casualty. But also, don't be a little wuss.

Send for Help: Calling for help or having someone call for help is important if available. Let's face it, first aid is just that: "first," not final, not most needed, just what you can provide in a situation you probably didn't anticipate. You are going to need backup for anything serious. The information you provide in this situation is important. First responders are primarily interested in the following information: situation, location, and type of injuries. This lets them know where to be, with how many, and what equipment.

Injury Assessment: This is where the good ole ABCs come into play. Step 1 is to try to identify the most life-threatening injury first. Someone could be in a situation where an injury is shocking but not life-threatening. Don't let a superficial bleed on the face distract you from an arterial bleed on the leg. Doing a quick visual inspection or pat down to feel for bleeding can be very important.

1. **Airway:** If their airway is obstructed, removing the obstruction is important, unless something is stuck in the airway. If they have something over their head or are choking, remove the obstacle or perform the Heimlich maneuver as needed. If something is actually stuck in the airway, such as a stabbing instrument or piece of debris, you're probably going to want to just secure it in place so as to prevent it from moving, not just pull it out, as that could cause additional bleeding and infection.

2. **Breathing:** You can check for breathing physically, audibly, and visually. If someone has no apparent obstruction to their airway but is not breathing, performing CPR or using a defibrillator may be your next step.

3. **Circulation (bleeding):** Stop the bleeding. Simple bleeds can be stopped by packing the injured space with an absorbent material and applying pressure. It may hurt them, but that's better than bleeding out. Bright red bleeding, often spurting, is a sign

of arterial bleeding, which you need to stop right away. Tourniquets can do long-term damage to limbs, but they are one of the best ways to stop an arterial bleed. You want some sort of strap capable of wrapping around the whole limb with enough left over, and usually two to three inches above the wound. Or if it is close to the joint, place the strap as close as possible, but on the other side of the joint and the wound. Take anything you can use as a lever and wrap the free end of the tourniquet to the lever (windlass or rod). You're going to twist the rod until the bleeding stops, or you can't twist it anymore. Then secure it to the limb so that the rod doesn't come loose. Remember to write down when the tourniquet was applied.

Basic first aid skills that are good to know: swimming, CPR, how to use an AED, making a tourniquet, knowledge of site assessment, triage, and individual assessment.

Basic first aid equipment that is good to have: tourniquet, gauze, medical tape, scissors, knife, bandages, water, and QuikClot.

Another good thing in an emergency is to keep your cool, convey instructions calmly and forcefully, and instill confidence in the people you are engaging with. If you are calm and in control, you will make the wounded person or people feel calm and be able to get instructions to the people who are helping.

LESSON 31

HOW TO BE THE HEAD OF YOUR HOUSEHOLD

How do you keep a marriage together forever?

I got asked this question on a plane once. It was a night flight, and I can't remember where I was going. I had just started reading a book when I noticed that the young woman sitting next to me had some papers out that she was trying to read in the dark because her overhead light wouldn't work.

I asked her if she would like to switch seats, since what she was trying to read looked a lot more time-sensitive than my book, and she was clearly relieved as she accepted.

Feeling the obligation that people do when accepting a favor, she explained that she was flying to a job interview and was reading up on the company and position. She had just gotten married, and this was an opportunity for both of them.

I told her that was great, and then I stopped and said, "Hey, I just want to tell you that marriage is great. I love being married, so congratulations!"

She immediately said, "Oh, thank you. How long have you been married?"

"Fourteen years." She was surprised. She didn't think I was that much older than her. Turns out I wasn't. About four years, if I remember correctly. With the kind of genuine curiosity that comes out in those unique situations where you have a question that's been bothering you, combined with a unique opportunity to ask someone with experience you will probably never see again, she asked, "How do you make it work?"

"Do you really want to know?"

This caused her to pause and kind of sheepishly say, "Uh . . . yes?"

"We have a biblical worldview of marriage."

"What does that mean?"

Now that was a very interesting reply. Once upon a time, people might have agreed, disagreed, smiled, gotten angry, or displayed any number of other reactions, but they would have known what I meant.

So, I began to explain things like how it provided a moral framework and guidance on the roles and responsibilities of husbands and wives, mothers and fathers. And then I said the thing that I was sure would end the conversation . . .

"It means I am the head of my family."

But to my surprise, she wasn't angry, just curious. "Why does someone need to be the head or in charge?"

What a great question! So, I asked her if when she got married, she and her husband said the typical lines about for better or for worse, in sickness and in health, till death do you part. She said they had.

"Did you mean it?"

"Yes."

"So, what happens when you have a disagreement that you can't find a compromise on? Who bears the responsibility for the decision?"

I then explained that my wife and I got married at nineteen and twenty. We had people at our wedding taking bets on how long we would last. Over the course of fourteen years, I had spent the equivalent of five years away from home between training, deployments, and combat. We had been poor, moved several times, had three kids, and worked through the issues that come with growing up in divorced households. In short, betting against us probably wasn't an outrageous idea. Still, in all that time, I could count on one hand the number of times we had to make a decision for which we could not come to a compromise.

In that moment, it was my responsibility to do what was best for the family. Not for myself, or my job, or my dreams and ambitions, but for them. If your household does not have a head, it still has someone making unilateral decisions, just without the accountability.

"Headship, in the Christian view of marriage, is not tyranny; it is responsibility and sacrifice. It is servant leadership. Yes, when we can't agree, one needs to submit to the other, but the price of that authority is sacrificing on behalf of my family, all the way and up to my life for theirs. That was the responsibility I agreed to when my wife said 'I do.' For the rest of my life, I have committed to being worthy of that role."

The young woman had never heard of that before. She proceeded to ask some more questions about communication and the roles we played. How we handled challenges, raising kids, and many of the typical questions a young married person asks someone who is a little farther along on the journey than they are. And then she thanked me.

She was an incredibly kind and inquisitive person who asked great questions and was willing to listen. You could tell she wanted her marriage to be successful and was willing to consider perspectives she had been completely unaware of before that conversation.

For me, it gave me an opportunity to articulate a lot of things I had thought about and tried to develop into concise explanations for what I believed and why.

She went on to finish reading the documents she needed to, I wished her good luck, and she thanked me for sharing my experiences.

I've reflected on that conversation many times since, whether I was sharing it with someone else or thinking about what I might have said better. I hope she got the job! Even more, I hope she and her husband have been happily married for the last eleven years!

> I tell this story not simply to have an opportunity to explain the concept behind servant leadership within marriage and what it means for a man, but to also point out that with experience comes a degree of responsibility. At a time when information is more available than ever, people feel saturated by it, without knowing what to actually trust. At some point in your life, you're going to need to share the wisdom you have learned. Sometimes because you got it right, and sometimes because you didn't. But don't be afraid to offer it. If not advice, let's say, then insight into decisions you made and how they worked out for you.

LESSON 32

HOW TO IMPROVE YOUR APPEARANCE

1. Shower regularly, guys.

2. Keep your hair properly groomed . . . wherever it is.

3. Your clothes don't have to be fancy.
   They just need to match and fit.

Most guides for "men" to look better start with instructions on how to buy $500 shoes and a cashmere cardigan. They are for males who pay someone else to mow their lawn.

I do not claim to be a fashion guru, but I have learned a few things along the way that will help you when it comes to managing your appearance, because it does matter. It's also not as hard as it seems.

So here are a few guidelines.

Hygiene REALLY matters: There are a lot of tricks and tips with respect to dress, and none of it will matter if you are dirty or smell, so with respect to hygiene, do the following.

1. **Shower regularly:** Showering is "as needed," but at a minimum aim for once a day because you should never go to bed dirty or sweaty unless, of course, you prefer a sexless marriage. And when you shower, be thorough. There was a disturbing trend on social media in 2024 of women asking their men if, when they showered, they washed in between their butt cheeks, and a lot of them said, "That's not a thing." Uhhh, yes, the hell it is! Being dirty because you have been working outside all day is perfectly natural; staying that way is lazy. And it's important to understand that "laziness" is what is conveyed. It's not just a bad aesthetic; it suggests a lack of discipline. I have a joke I tell where I say, "If I want to treat my wife, I'll get all gussied up, put on a sport coat, and take her to dinner. But if I want to seduce my wife, I put on a cowboy hat and do about three hours of yard work." And while it's true that this does in fact work every time, as much as she likes the aesthetic of her man after working in the sun, nothing is happening until I get a shower.

2. **Manage your hair . . . all of it:** Regular haircuts are important. Finding a barber or stylist who knows your hair and will provide a consistent cut is a way to achieve that. Also, depending on your style, product is your friend. I resisted putting gel in my hair for a long time, but for my hair in particular, it makes a big difference, and my wife likes it, so I

do it. Also, trim your nose, ear, and eyebrow hair if necessary. It's not that hard, and you can do it with a twelve-dollar trimmer. Nose and ear hair are not attractive. When you get older and you're dealing with back hair, trim it. An easy way to do it yourself is with a BakBlade. Again, there is no universe where back hair is desirable. The other thing I will mention is chest and armpit hair. My wife is the kind of woman who thinks a man should have chest hair. But that doesn't mean it has to be unruly. So, keep it trimmed to what your wife likes.

3. **Nails:** Keep your nails trimmed and clean. Easy enough. People notice hands, but toenails still matter.

4. **Skin care:** This is where I get hypocritical, so do as I say, not as I have done, but for the love of all that is holy, use sunscreen. It's also not a bad idea to have something of a regular regime when it comes to skin care, especially on your face, since it generally sees the most sun and gets the most damage. I'm not saying you have to spend an hour before the mirror every morning, but taking a little time to protect your skin is a good investment.

Dress and attire: I was not a kid who grew up with designer clothing, and for much of my adult life, I have resisted spending much on clothing for myself. I say this right off the bat because I understand that it's easy to "dress nice" when you have a massive budget, but what about when you don't? You don't have to dress expensively to look put together. But there are some simple guidelines to follow.

1. **Fitting:** Clothes that fit properly go a long way. This is going to sound like a shameless plug because they advertise with me. But long before I ever had a brand deal with True Classic, I loved their clothing. Primarily because of their T-shirts, which to this day are my preferred clothing and fit perfectly. Tighter in the shoulders, chest, and arms, with a little more give around the waist, which means they are comfortable AND look good. Having clothes that properly fit your body type also makes you look more put together, which, again, conveys more to people than just an aesthetic; it suggests attention to detail.

2. **Matching belt and shoes:** Brown shoes, brown belt. Black shoes, black belt. It's really that simple. Also, if you are on a budget, make sure that you have a belt and shoes that you wear only for more formal events. This will ensure that belts and shoes don't look overly worn. If you need it, a little bit of shoe polish can go a long way in sprucing them up.

3. **Developing a style:** I do not particularly enjoy dressing formally, or even semiformally, for that matter. But when I started getting involved in politics in Virginia, it was no longer an option. I noticed that every male Virginia politician I saw would always wear what I called the "Virginia Politician's Uniform": blue blazer, brass buttons, khakis, and loafers. I remember hating that look so much that I even mentioned it when I was asked to run for office. "Okay, but I'm NEVER wearing that." So, I came up with my own look.

Cowboy boots, unfaded blue jeans, a button-down shirt, and a sport coat. I started calling it "Culpeper Black Tie." It was a little less formal because of the blue jeans, but it still looked put together, and honestly, it looked more masculine. It caught on, and now "Culpeper Black Tie" is a thing in this area. The key to developing a style is picking something that works with your personality while still looking put together. Had I worn dirty jeans or messed-up work boots, it wouldn't have worked. But whatever your style, remember that circumstances and occasion still matter. Create something that works within your environment, not something that is flippant or insulting toward it.

These are just very basic tips, but they are important. It's okay to say that looks and style don't matter if you plan to work in a monastery, but for everyone else, it matters.

LESSON 33

HOW TO LEAD IN YOUR MARRIAGE

"Your wife wants you to lead."

Strong women want stronger men.

Yeah, I said it. Your wife actually wants you to be the head of the household, to lead, to be able to even . . . gasp . . . "submit" to you.

Should I give everyone a chance to take a couple of deep breaths, maybe look over your shoulder and make sure no one catches you reading this line, and think you actually agree with it?

It's true. Maybe not in all cases, but I believe it is in the vast majority. Nothing about this statement should be used to imply that this somehow makes women weak or inferior to men. It's just a highly controversial statement of fact that, when recognized and respected, leads to happier and more stable marriages.

I married a very strong, very opinionated, very capable woman. She had to spend a lot of time running everything without me, including managing the home, raising kids, fixing things around the house, and a lot of other things, while I was off gallivanting around the world fighting wars, training Korean special ops one minute and Bangladeshi border guards the next.

We had bad water, needed a major water filtration system, and couldn't afford it . . . she figured it out.

We decided we didn't like what was going on in the public school system and chose to educate at home three children with very different strengths, goals, and challenges . . . she figured it out.

We decided to pack up and move to the other side of the country, where we knew almost no one and had no family support . . . she figured it out.

I can safely say that if I died tomorrow, Tina would be sad. But bills would get paid, the grass would get mowed, the kids would be provided for, and life would go on. Because my wife is a strong woman who, in a very real sense, "don't need no man."

But she wanted one. She wanted a husband and a father for her children. She wanted a man she could go through life with, trust, care for, and yes, depend on. And she wanted that man to be strong. To be someone she could be proud of and feel safe with. And because of who she was, I wanted to be that man. Not just before we got married, or after our wedding, or after we had kids. I want to be that man right now. I want to be him tomorrow.

I'm going to drag my ass out of bed tomorrow and go to the gym, go to work, research, study, pray, and continue to work on myself spiritually, physically, intellectually, emotionally, and professionally so that I can be the kind of man who represents all the things she ever wanted or needed in a man.

Be a leader worth following. Be that for her. She deserves it. And you will both be happier for it.

That doesn't mean that all wives or women acknowledge that. If you are dating someone who is adamant that they "don't need a man" or insists that you take their name, you're going to want to be careful about marrying them. Not because they are the only woman in the world who doesn't actually want their husband to lead, but because they have bought into the lie that they shouldn't want or need it. This means they will be disappointed when you try to be that leader and even more disappointed when you don't. It's a lose-lose, brother.

But how you lead matters. Servant leadership is the goal. The kind of leadership that commands respect because it is rooted in competence, honor, and service. Nobody wants just anybody to "lead them." But everyone thrives under effective leadership, so strive to be that.

In short: An intelligent, emotionally and spiritually mature, strong and capable husband is easy for your wife to follow.

LESSON 34

HOW TO CRAFT A LOGICAL ARGUMENT

1. Understand the laws of logic.

2. Understand the structure of arguments.

3. Understand how to identify fallacies and why they are fallacies.

It's unfortunate that the word *argument* has taken on such a negative connotation in modern society. According to *Merriam-Webster*, *argumentation* is "the act or process of forming reasons and of drawing conclusions and applying them to a case in discussion."

That doesn't sound so bad.

Oxford describes it as "the action or process of reasoning systematically in support of an idea, action, or theory."

Even better!

When you look up *arguing* or *argue*, you can also get something like this: exchange or express diverging or opposite views, typically in a heated or angry way.

Let's try our best to avoid engaging in that third version if possible. And to do that, we need to lay out the groundwork for what constitutes a "good argument."

Good argumentation comes with some rules. Things to include and things to avoid. The foundation for good argumentation starts with the laws of logic.

There are three traditional laws of logic.

1. **The Law of Identity:** This simply means that if a statement is true, it is true, or "what is, is." That sounds redundant, but another way to think about it is if the statement is "true" in the argument, that is because it is true in reality. Example: A nonvenomous snake is, by definition, a snake that does not possess venom.

2. **The Law of Noncontradiction:** Contradictory propositions cannot both be true in the same sense at the same time. Another way of putting it is "nothing can both be and not be." Example: The statement that the car is blue and the car is not blue cannot be true if we are talking about the same car at the same time.

3. **The Law of the Excluded Middle:** For every proposition, either this proposition or its negation is true. Another way to put it is "everything must either be or not be." This is what I now call the "screw your multiverse plot contrivance" rule. Example: We are both watching a football game, but then I insist that it is actually a baseball game. After you painstakingly explain the fundamental differences for why we cannot be watching a baseball game, I then suggest that perhaps somewhere in the

multiverse a different version of us is watching a baseball game . . . and so I'm right. I have just violated the Law of the Excluded Middle by suggesting some alternate reality where my contradictory statement could maybe, kinda, be potentially correct. I would be wrong . . . but I could probably get a job green-lighting scripts for Marvel movies.

There are, of course, some people who will object to these or suggest that there are others, but for the vast majority of the world, these three laws provide the foundational principles for engaging in effective argumentation.

Next, let's look into logical reasoning.

Logical reasoning is an intellectual process that aims to arrive at correct conclusions through sound processes.

Arguments are built upon premises and inferences.

A premise is a true or false declarative statement.

And inference is a conclusion reached on the basis of evidence or reasoning.

Logical reasoning is broken down into two broad forms of argumentation, deductive and nondeductive.

Deductive argumentation is one in which, if the premises are true, the conclusion must be true.

1. Premise 1: All men are mortal.

2. Premise 2: Socrates is a man.

3. Inference: Socrates is mortal.

You can see here how if the two premises are true, then the inference MUST be true.

This part is interesting . . . deductive arguments are not just graded on whether they are correct. They are graded first for validity and then for being "sound" or "unsound." The grade for validity has to do with the structure of the argument. If the inference naturally follows from the two premises or statements offered, then the argument is a valid deductive argument, but that doesn't mean it is "correct" or "sound."

Here is an example of a valid deductive argument that is unsound.

1. Premise 1: All politicians are idiots.

2. Premise 2: George Washington was a politician.

3. Inference: George Washington was an idiot.

The structure of this argument is valid in the sense that if premise 1 and premise 2 are in fact true, then the inference MUST be true. But unless you're a history professor at Cal Berkeley, you probably do not agree that George Washington was an idiot simply because he was a politician. So, this deductive argument is valid, but unsound.

Perhaps the most important thing to understand about deductive reasoning is that if the argument is both valid and sound, then the inference or conclusion MUST be true.

Now let's look at nondeductive arguments.

Nondeductive arguments usually fall into one of three categories: inductive, abductive, or analogical.

Inductive arguments infer a universal law from patterns found in individual cases. Example: Every time I push the starter on my grill, the propane ignites so that I can cook meat. If I push the starter on my grill tomorrow, it will light the propane so that I can cook meat.

Abductive is also known as "inference to the best explanation" and starts from making an observation and then reasoning to the fact or facts that explain the observation. Example: I see cooked meat sitting right next to the grill and conclude that the grill had something to do with cooking the meat.

Analogical reasoning is the process of analyzing two similar systems and concluding that if one of them has a feature, then the other will as well. Example: I see a propane grill sitting next to mine and conclude that the other grill includes a mechanism like mine for using propane to cook meat.

Right now, you are probably concluding that I wanted steak as I was writing this. That would be a form of abductive reasoning. That would be both strong and cogent . . . which leads us to our next point.

Nondeductive arguments are graded differently than deductive arguments because nondeductive arguments don't ensure "truth" but provide a conclusion that is convincing or highly likely to be "true."

Nondeductive arguments can be strong or weak, and then cogent or uncogent.

A "strong" nondeductive argument means the premises, if true, lead to a high degree of probability that the inference or conclusion is true.

Cogent is when the premises are actually true.

1. Premise 1: Every time it rains, my lawn floods.

2. Premise 2: It's raining right now.

3. Inference: My lawn has probably flooded.

This is an example of a strong nondeductive argument. It is not a guarantee that my lawn flooded. For instance, it's possible someone could have conducted maintenance that I am not aware of, which allowed for better draining. When I pull into my driveway and discover that my lawn is in fact flooded, I now know that my nondeductive argument was BOTH strong AND cogent . . . dang it. If I showed up and my lawn wasn't flooded, my argument still would have been strong, but not cogent, as there was another piece of data that I was missing when I put my premises together.

So, what does an example of a weak argument look like?

1. Premise 1: Mom never lets me do anything.

2. Premise 2: I want to do something.

3. Inference: Mom probably won't let me.

It's highly unlikely that premise 1 is actually true. It may feel like that, but the odds that this is a true statement as opposed to just hyperbole are highly unlikely. Now go clean your room.

> NOTE: The main takeaway from all of this is that deduction arguments seek to provide "certainty" and nondeductive arguments seek to provide a "high degree of probability."

Why does any of this matter?

While discussing all of this might seem complicated, we actually do it every day without really thinking about it. Every time you put your key in the ignition and turn it over, you are engaging in inductive reasoning. You didn't walk out to your car and conduct a series of tests to determine whether the various rules governing physics were still in play before jumping to the radical conclusion that the thing you do every day would, in fact, work this day as well. You just did it. And it probably worked. Now let's say one morning it doesn't. You probably will not come to the deductive conclusion that if your key didn't work this morning, that must mean that the laws of physics no longer apply to your car. You will most likely assume that there is something wrong based on what happens.

Key didn't fit . . . you grabbed the wrong keys.

Key fit but didn't turn over . . . battery is probably dead.

Key fit, turned over, but the car exploded . . . you angered the mob.

It's pretty amazing how God created our minds to go through these processes, and while attempting to write out all the processes, or even more confounding to me, putting them in mathematical language, can be confusing, we actually use them without even thinking about it. Until it gets to politics, and then we throw them right out the window.

In the next chapter, we will talk about all the glorious ways we do that!

LESSON 35

HOW TO CRAFT AN EFFECTIVE ARGUMENT

1. Understand logic and structured arguments.

2. Be able to identify fallacies.

3. Understand that fallacies often work because they give the listener what they want.

4. Listen before speaking.

5. Instead of "defeating" the other person, leave them better informed or more empowered as a result of uncovering a truth they didn't previously see or understand.

We've talked about logical arguments and how to spot fallacious arguments; now it's time to discuss how to craft "effective" arguments.

"But Nick, if our argument is logical, doesn't that make it

effective?" NO. If only that were so. There are people right now creating effective arguments that possess some of the most twisted logic I have ever seen. Case in point, there are judges in California right now deciding (custody) cases that allow for children as young as ten to undergo expensive and life-altering "medical treatment" designed to "affirm" not their gender but their dysphoria.

These people are literally chemically altering their child's natural and healthy development based on a mental break with biological reality.

How logically and empirically rigorous do you find the arguments in favor of surgically altering teenagers by cutting off perfectly healthy organs?

One of the biggest problems we have in the conservative, libertarian, and Christian communities is an inability to make effective arguments.

So, how do we correct that? Do we throw out logic and go for the emotional appeal like so many of our intellectual opponents do?

No. It is incredibly important that sound reason and sufficient evidence always be sought out when formulating a position or policy. Emotional arguments devoid of these components may work in convincing people, but they always end up failing one way or another, usually leaving a lot of injured people in their wake.

By the same token, logical arguments devoid of emotion can often appear heartless or so singularly focused on one perspective that they ignore others, sometimes very important ones, necessary to understanding the whole picture.

When you have a visceral or emotional response to something (remember, guys, anger is an emotion), understand that it is an invitation to thought. Someone who acts on an emotion without really considering the problem is either incredibly impulsive or not as caring as they present themselves to be. By that I mean, genuinely caring people are concerned about properly diagnosing a problem and then addressing it in the way that best solves it. Many people who present themselves as compassionate often have ulterior motives, or their primary concern is not genuinely addressing the needs of others but alleviating their own angst or desiring to appear virtuous.

Here are some ways to properly bridge the gap between the emotional and the intellectual when addressing an issue. Identify the problem everyone is trying to solve. Analyze the problem from multiple perspectives, assessing potential causes, incentive structures, and the individuals affected. Begin by formulating possible approaches to the problem, considering how incentive structures might be altered, who will be affected by the changes, who is responsible for implementing or enforcing them, and what the potential second- and third-order effects may be.

This sounds like a long process, and it can be, but you may be surprised at how quickly you will conclude that in many cases, the solution seldom includes the government doing more.

LESSON 36

HOW TO ADMIT YOU'RE WRONG TO YOUR KIDS

1. Teach them about objective standards of right and wrong.

2. Live them out as best you can; no one is perfect.

3. Allow a space where your children can challenge an action respectfully.

4. Praise them when they both have the courage to challenge authority AND do it respectfully.

I'll never forget the time I came home from work and found that my two youngest children had destroyed the kitchen. It was an absolute mess. I was already stressed out from work, so I went off. I yelled at them both. I wasn't interested in any explanation. Just clean it up and go to your rooms.

About ten minutes later, my oldest daughter, who was about

thirteen at the time, knocked on the door and said, "Daddy, is now an okay time to talk to you for a minute?" I told her it was, and she proceeded to tell me that she didn't think I had handled the situation very well. Now think about this. I'm already mad, I'm frustrated about a number of different things, and I feel completely justified in being frustrated about coming home to what looked like a failed science experiment in the kitchen. Now my thirteen-year-old is informing me that I didn't handle that well.

Every ounce of me wanted to remind her that this was my house, I provided for her entire existence, and if I needed help with raising children from someone, it would not be from a thirteen-year-old. However, she had asked if now was a good time to talk. She hadn't yelled across the hallway. She hadn't barged into my room. She didn't knock on the door and say, "What was that, Dad!?" She had waited ten minutes, given me time to cool down, and then politely asked if I had time to talk with her. So instead of blowing up, I asked her to explain.

She went on to tell me that my two younger children had asked Mommy for permission to make me something as a surprise. They had been working on it in anticipation of my getting home, and instead of getting to surprise me, they were both in their rooms, sad, because I was so angry. They were now afraid to tell me what was going on and why.

You can imagine how I felt. I ended up thanking my daughter for telling me. I complimented her on having the courage to come to me and politely and respectfully explain what happened, and to be honest with me. I apologized to her and to my son and youngest daughter.

Hard truths have to work both ways.

Teaching your children that there is an objective standard for truth, for right and wrong, means that when you fall short of it, you have to accept correction.

Now, you may be thinking that this is important from a simple position of honesty and consistency, and you would be right. But it's more than that. The reason a moment like this is so important is that it reaffirms to your children the rules you taught them. The morality that you raised them with is objective, not arbitrary. Right and wrong are not right and wrong because Mommy and Daddy say so. It's not that way simply because I have the ability to impose my will. It's not that way because I have the ability to punish dissent and reward obedience. Something is right or wrong because it's part of God's created order.

If your child catches you violating the very rules of morality you impose upon them, you change the nature of the argument and make it all about "your house, your rules." Well then, don't be surprised when they abandon "your rules" the moment it's not "your house."

Perhaps one of the many reasons we have so many kids who quickly abandon their parents' values when they go off to college or enter the workforce is not because "that's their rebellious phase" but because they were never taught "values." What they were taught was an authority structure that rewarded obedience and punished dissent. And the moment the person wielding power changed, so did their allegiance.

If you want your kids to have the courage of their convictions, then a few things are going to have to be demonstrated for them.

1. You have to teach your kids right and wrong and explain why something is a moral imperative rather than just a preference.

2. You have to both model the standard for your kids as well as adequately equip them to defend it. It has to become their conviction, not just yours.

3. If they catch you violating the rule, own up to it.

That last one is important for another reason. It teaches them how to properly question authority. If you want a child who can stand up to peer pressure, a professor, a boss, or a politician, they have to have been taught how to do that. And it may just start when they catch you.

> Just to be clear, I'm not suggesting that if your child goes out of their way to embarrass you when you get something wrong that you should put up with it. I reacted the way I did to my daughter not because she challenged me but because she did so with respect. There have been other times when one of my kids questioned something at an inappropriate time or had misread a situation, and I made it very clear that the manner in which they went about challenging me was disrespectful and rude. When I did, they backed down for two reasons. One, they knew I would explain to them what my reasoning was for something. Two, a pattern had already been established: I could admit being wrong if I was in fact wrong.

LESSON 37

HOW TO DEFEND YOUR FAITH

First sanctify Christ in your heart and always be prepared to give an answer for the hope that is in you. But do so with gentleness and respect, keeping a clear conscience, so that those who speak maliciously against your good behavior in Christ may be ashamed of their slander.

—1 Peter 3:15–16

This is sometimes referred to as the "Apologist's verse." I quote it a lot, almost as much as I fall short of it. It reminds me that while God does not need me to defend my faith, He does command me to, and He has a specific way He wants it done.

I am going to lay out what I believe to be a simple yet convincing argument for Christianity. But first, let's define some terms.

I first started really getting into Christian apologetics in 2007. This is not to say that I had never studied the concept of defending one's faith before then, but that is when it became a more serious study for me. And it has been incredibly important to my faith. But let me issue a couple of warnings up front.

1. **Christianity is not purely an intellectual pursuit. It's a relationship.** That's not some kind of cop-out to get out of answering tough questions. It's just a fact. As Michael Ramsden once put it, someone might be able to give me a very intellectually rigorous argument for why my wife doesn't exist. One that I do not possess an answer to in the moment. But that doesn't mean I will instantly stop believing in my wife, because I have a relationship with her. It's supposed to be the same with God. It is because I believe in the truth of Christianity that I am always willing to hear arguments against it. I have faith that there are answers, and I have never been disappointed. I have certainly been temporarily perplexed, confused, stumped, and even angry at times. But there has always been an answer. So, keep seeking the truth.

2. **I appreciate the work of great apologists. But they are not who I follow.** I have learned a great deal from Christian apologists who failed in one or more aspects of their lives. One in particular who had been very influential in my thinking stumbled hard. I was asked if those failures "shook my faith." No. Why would they? I appreciated that man's ability to make an argument for Christianity, but I never confused him with Christ. All that to say, apologetics is ultimately about serving God, not following a particular approach, an apologist, or a winning argument.

So, why is defending the faith important?

First of all, because Christianity includes "loving the Lord your God with all your mind," this applies to both how you think about things and your desire to better understand what you believe. Christians started modern science because they believed that God was a God of order and had created things in such a way for us to discover more about our world—and through that, its Creator.

If you think about it, every truly meaningful relationship you have includes the intellectual. Why would a relationship with God be any different? Understanding what you believe and why is important not only for those who ask you questions but for your own relationship with God. Apologetics is not just about getting better at arguing for what you believe, but getting better at understanding what you believe through contemplation and rigorous analysis.

Second, apologetics has an evangelical component to it. There are those who are earnestly trying to make sense of a complex, confusing, and often evil world, and they want to understand if there is any ultimate purpose, meaning, or reason for what they see and feel. You are going to want to be able to answer those questions with more than just platitudes.

Even if you are arguing with an avowed atheist, your points could be heard by someone open to the message or a believer who needs the encouragement right now.

One hundred and fifty years ago, it would have seemed utterly ridiculous to assume that someone lacked intelligence because they believed in God. It's time to make it ridiculous again, but if we are to do that, Christians need to treat their faith like it deserves, instead of like a fad diet or lousy "self-help" regimen.

So, here are some things I have learned concerning what we might call "general apologetics."

Many of the arguments against Christianity rely on presuppositions that cannot even be sustained within the atheistic worldview. Morality, evil, goodness, ultimate meaning or purpose, and even truth cannot be sustained in any objective fashion within atheism. Your casual atheist will challenge this, and your intellectually rigorous atheist will brag about it.

Let's discuss some of these.

Objective morality is the belief that there are some things, feelings, or actions that are objectively good or evil. There has to be a standard by which these things can be judged. Religion provides such a standard because it offers an objective moral lawgiver. Without an objective moral lawgiver, all you have is either consensus, power (which can be another form of consensus), or utilitarianism (if it "works," it's "good" or, rather, "useful").

Evil assumes that an action is not just "less than useful." It invokes a moral category about what "ought" to happen (or not happen). A world where there is no authoritative moral lawgiver cannot have universal objective moral categories. You can only have agreed-upon moral precepts. Even if you try and suggest that "morality" exists as a result of biological evolution designed to improve the propagation of the species, that doesn't achieve what some atheists think it does. For instance, if propagation of the species is the ultimate moral imperative under an atheistic framework, then rape may be an acceptable or even desirable action, if it "propagates the species." Even if atheists conclude that rape is not desirable for other reasons, they still can't say it is "wrong," only less desirable from a utilitarian perspective. But what if the utilitarian circumstances change? Then is it okay? The best the atheist can offer is "Well, I can't say it's objectively wrong, because I don't think such categories exist, but I would never do that." Good luck ever getting a date again after you say that in public.

Sometimes the casual atheist will respond with something like "I don't need God to tell me that evil things shouldn't be done. So, if there were no God, you would just go around raping people?"

While this particular atheist and I agree it's wrong, what we need is for all humans to agree that rape is always wrong, which is not the state of the world today. That a rule is universally applicable is the difference between an objective moral law and just a feeling some people have.

If objective morality is dependent upon an ultimate objective authority and such an authority doesn't exist, then you may not "need God" to tell you not to rape someone, but you do need Him to classify it as objectively wrong. Otherwise, all we are left with is majority rules or everyone just makes up their own morality. Both of which come with significant moral hazards. If a society were to adopt slavery as a legal form of property, I'm guessing the casual atheist wouldn't say, "Well, the majority has spoken." They would claim that it was wrong. Okay, by what standard? Tradition? Slavery was a tradition throughout human history across space, time, and people groups. Or would they claim, based on their "individual morality," it was wrong?

I once had a woman tell me she didn't need God to discern right from wrong. I asked her what she used. She said that if she could get up in the morning and look at herself in the mirror and know she was a good person, that was enough. I told her that sounded a little psychopathic. She angrily asked me if I had any idea what a psychopath was actually like. I said, "It's someone who can justify their actions based on no higher authority than whether or not they can look themselves in the mirror and feel like a good person." Psychopaths ignore objective or even communal moral laws in favor of their own individualized ones. If an action benefits them, it's justified.

Then you will get the "utilitarian" case, which is to say that if an action is useful, we may call it "good." Okay. Useful for what? An individual, a group, the majority? If killing and taking stuff from 49 percent of the people and giving it to 51 percent of the people is useful for the majority, is it justified?

The bottom line is that no matter what alternative you provide for God-given objective morality, you are going to end up with something arbitrary, unpredictable, and different all over.

It turns out the vast majority of us don't live our lives as if such a reality were true, regardless of what we claim. Even the people who diligently argue that there is no such thing as objective morality believe that they have been "wronged" when they are stolen from or beaten up. You could try telling yourself that this is just social engineering . . . or maybe it's an indicator that there is, in fact, such a thing as objective morality, and understanding who the author of such a reality is and why they have set things up the way they have could be a pretty important thing to figure out.

As I've pointed out before, most people are perfectly capable of driving a car without understanding the finer points of the physics and engineering that make an internal combustion engine work. But it would be pretty ridiculous to suggest that it works simply because we have a consensus that it works.

Go to any college campus, and you will find a surprisingly large number of students going into debt who are willing to argue with you about this fact. They may claim that "truth is subjective" or that we all have "our truth." This is perhaps the easiest concept to destroy by asking one question.

The next time you hear someone say that there is no "truth," ask them if that is true.

If it's true that there is no truth . . . then they're wrong about there being no such thing as truth.

If it isn't true that there is no such thing as truth . . . then why listen to them? They just told you they were lying.

"Ah, but Nick, what if they say they don't know?"

Ask them if it is true that they don't know.

"Okay, but what if they say that's their truth?"

Ask them if it is true that that is "their truth."

Here is the bottom line. It's an inherently contradictory statement. IF you believe "each of us can be moral according to our own values," that is still a universal truth. So where did they get THAT universal truth?

Just like objective morality, we all operate as if there were an objective truth. All of physical science is predicated on the idea that we can make observations about reality and come to rational conclusions about how things operate. None of which would be possible if "truth were subjective."

It's not that they have attained some heightened level of "consciousness or awareness." They're engaging in nonsense at worst and conflation at best.

It is true that each of us may have a different "perspective" on the truth, but perspective and truth are not necessarily the same thing. We intuitively understand this because when a car accident happens, the investigation usually includes getting multiple perspectives on what happened in order to try and draw a complete picture, not of "our truth" but "the truth." There is still an objective truth about what happened in the accident.

Conflating perspective with truth is a category error. The only reason this absurd idea gains any traction is because it offers people something we have wanted ever since the Garden of Eden. Namely, the ability to define and live by "our own truth." Which we find out we don't like very much as someone with a similar belief mugs us.

Meaning and purpose are what we call our desire to know the meaning of life and what our specific role is.

Again, the best an atheistic framework can give us is that you are here by cosmic accident, nothing you do matters in any eternal sense, and when you die, you are worm food. Soooo, live it up, I guess? But the problem is that the people who interpret "live it up" usually do so in a hedonistic way. Others will try to find meaning in helping alleviate the suffering of other cosmic accidents, who will one day be worm food. Which one is better? Well, with no objective morality to go off of, I can tell you what most people will choose.

And yet, we do desire a greater meaning and purpose to our lives. Why? Is it just wishful thinking? Maybe an evolutionary drive? For what? Why? Are we all just doomed to search for an ultimate meaning and purpose that doesn't ultimately exist? Or is it more likely that billions of people through history have sought meaning and purpose because we were created to?

Maybe you disagree with that. Maybe you think it is simplistic. Personally, I think it is simplistic and rather depressing to believe that it's all just in our heads. That's quite the coincidence.

So why did we just go through all of this?

Because at the heart of the questions we have about God are the questions of truth, morality, purpose, and meaning.

Far from being just a scam or wishful thinking about Sky Daddy, Christianity answers these questions in a way that not only makes a great deal of sense intellectually but also answers our next level of questions concerning love, justice, forgiveness, and reconciliation.

Is it really just a cosmic coincidence that we seem to be the only creatures in the known universe obsessed with love and justice?

Love might be defined as a deep and sacrificial attachment to someone or something. Justice may be defined as the right thing, happening for the right reasons, at the right time.

We don't just desire to be "desired" for our physical beauty or what we can provide; we desire to be genuinely loved and to love genuinely.

We don't just desire things; we actually desire justice. We want to feel that we have earned what we have. And we want the purveyors of injustice to be punished and the victims of injustice to be made whole.

By the same token, we want to believe in forgiveness and reconciliation, because we all know of times when we have been the purveyors of injustice and deeply desired an opportunity for forgiveness and reconciliation.

Now, let us engage in a thought exercise.

Let us assume that there is such a thing as love in this world. What does love require to be genuine in nature?

It requires choice.

To genuinely love someone, you have to choose to. Because love in its purest form is not only attraction but a willingness to sacrifice to benefit them, it's the willingness that gives it meaning.

So, how does a just God, author of morality and truth, enter into a loving relationship with His creation? He gives us a choice. Not unlimited choice. We are not the Creator and therefore do not have the power to change the nature of existence, truth, or morality. But we can choose whom we wish to interact with it. This is the only environment where love, as we understand it, can exist.

If we are forced to "love" God, we are robots incapable of love the way God experiences it within the Trinity.

So, God in the garden gives us life, truth, morality, companionship, meaning, purpose, and love. He also gives us one rule. Do not eat of the fruit of the knowledge of good and evil. He gives us everything we think we could possibly want with only one simple rule to follow.

We break it. Why? We were convinced by one question and a competing claim.

The question was "Did God really say . . . ?" followed by "If you eat of it, you will become like God."

Now you may say, "Nick, what is all this 'we' stuff? I was never in the garden." To which I ask . . . which of us hasn't rejected God's truth, out of a desire to do the opposite, which can be explained only by our desire to make our own rules?

But I'll ask it another way: Can you acknowledge that you have done bad things in your life? Lying, cheating, stealing, covetousness, greed, jealousy, maybe something worse?

If the answer is yes, then you're guilty. I know I am.

LESSON 38

HOW TO INTIMIDATE YOUR DAUGHTER'S DATE

Your daughter probably doesn't want you to beat up her boyfriend. However, she wants to know you would, and she needs to know you could.

Apparently, this statement is about an eight on the toxic masculinity scale, according to single women on Instagram. If I'm being generous, I can understand how someone might be concerned that this is an overly aggressive remark. But here is the question for anyone willing to seriously consider it.

Is it true?

Would your daughter prefer to believe that, should her boyfriend ever make her feel physically unsafe, there is nothing Dad could do about it, except maybe call some other man to take a police report? Would she prefer a reality where even if Dad was able to do something, he refused to, because that sort of aggression is "toxic"?

I'm sure the proper answer is she would prefer to live in a world where such violence wasn't necessary. Okay, sure, but do we? Do the people who have a problem with this statement believe the world will get better if good men are incapable or unwilling to utilize violence against bad men? Is that likely to get us closer to the sort of world where bad things just "don't happen"?

I doubt it. Furthermore, I'm not going to risk it.

Anybody who chooses to read what I wrote in good faith can probably surmise that I'm not saying that dads should go around randomly beating up their daughter's boyfriend. If you are threatening teenage boys to make yourself feel tough, or just to embarrass your kid, you are a jerk. However, not every polite varsity athlete with a hint of a mustache is polite when you're not around. Your daughter needs to be secure enough in her father's love for her and his capability to protect her that it makes sense to run to him if things get sketchy.

It's amazing to me that the same people claiming that 25 percent of women will get sexually assaulted on a college campus think it's horribly toxic for a father to be physically protective of his daughter.

Any woman who wants a man to walk her to her car in the dark would be foolish to turn down a father who likes to vet the other men who would walk her to a car in the dark.

I have actually gotten along very well with potential suitors for my daughters, and I now have a great son-in-law. But you better believe that they understood that my daughters were under my protection, and should their intentions stray into the "not honorable" category, they would, without a shadow of a doubt, meet a very different Mr. Freitas than the one they were accustomed to. If they had had a problem with that, I would have considered it a major red flag.

LESSON

HOW TO SET UP A DATE

I'm going to be honest, I hesitated to write this one, but I had some people ask me for it, so here it is.

I got married at nineteen, and I just don't have much dating experience for obvious reasons. However, I have learned a few things through trial and error, as well as through honest conversations with my wife, so I provide some basic guidelines here.

Getting to know someone outside romantic intent can be incredibly valuable in order to determine whether someone is a possible spouse, likely friend, or crazy person to run from. Better to have some indication of which category they fall into BEFORE going on a date. I'm not saying blind dates can't work or that you have to know someone incredibly well before asking them out. It is just that a "date" is, by its very nature, a romance-oriented encounter. If there isn't a second one, people feel rejected. If it takes four or five dates before you realize this was a horrible mistake, if both of you were putting on a charade that was only revealed two months in, then you have both wasted your time.

Getting to know someone in group settings, preferably with

groups or at events where you have a high degree of certainty that the people there will share your worldview, is ideal before asking someone out.

But let's be real about what dating is.

Not to make this weird, but what each of you is engaged in is an intelligence-gathering operation and a bit of psychological operations. Because you are both there, that means you are both looking to see if a longer relationship is possible. That means both of you are gathering information and putting out information that paints you in a good light. It's not necessarily subversive or anything. That's just human nature.

So, understand what that means. You are looking for indicators for whether you should pursue a relationship. Both of you have an incentive to put the best versions of yourselves forward. But you don't need the best version. You need the truth. So, how do you achieve that?

The first date is "deductive" in nature. That means you both should be looking for indicators of disqualifications, so you don't pursue something that shouldn't be. This means you need to set up an environment that is comfortable and safe, and allows you to have not only small talk but meaningful conversations. So, how do you do that when people don't necessarily want to reveal things about themselves?

You focus on conversational topics that are safe, but provide indicators. Learning about where someone is from, their family, hopes, dreams, and ambitions are all pretty safe topics for a first date and can provide a lot of useful information.

If, during the conversation, it becomes apparent that she used to be "such a party girl" or she is really enjoying majoring in "gender studies" with classes on the "historical benefits of polyamory," you might have your answer for the price of a single meal!

Some people will throw out red flags like a "bad relationship with her father." To which I will tell you, there is a big difference between things that happen to a person and how they handle them. An estranged family life may be an "indicator" but not necessarily in the way you think. At my wife's and my wedding, there were two types of people. Those who really wanted us to make it, and those who were betting on how long we would last. Nobody was willing to bet the farm on two kids, nineteen and twenty, with no money, who both came from broken homes, going the distance. But here we are, and the people betting against us ended up divorced.

Some people are understandably broken by the trauma they experienced, and others let it inform them in ways that make them strong. I'm not suggesting anyone ignore indicators that might suggest future issues. However, understanding how someone copes with hardship, disappointment, and tragedy may be one of the most important things you can know about a person before committing to them for life.

I know that I'm making this sound more like an espionage scenario than a romantic setting, but let's be honest . . . how much "romance" do you want to have with someone before you actually know them? A lot of what modernity calls "romance" is little more than camouflaged lust. Romance should be spent on the person we love, and you can't do that without first knowing them.

Let's look at the mechanics.

SCENARIO 1: FIRST DATE WITH SOMEONE YOU DON'T REALLY KNOW

So, if you ignored everything I just said and asked someone out purely on looks and maybe some shared interests, you should avoid the urge to try to go too romantic on a first date. I really can't stress this enough: Big romantic gestures are for someone you have a relationship with, not an attempt to impress someone you don't. Otherwise, what you think is "romantic" can get you thrown into the "creep" zone very quick.

You shouldn't be "cooking her dinner" at your place, because you have no idea what kind of allergies, food preferences, or anything else she has, not to mention you are not selecting a place that offers "neutral ground" or a sense of safety, since you are essentially still a stranger.

By the same token, don't make her plan the date. Regardless of what modern feminism tells men about women—or women about women, for that matter—she does want to see a man who is competent and can make a decision.

So, select a nice restaurant that has a decent variety of options and good reviews. That way, if there are any issues with things like food allergies or diets, she can be accommodated. Also, pick something you can afford. Don't let the understandable desire to make a "good first impression" turn into something you can't sustain. Make a good first impression based on your character, intelligence, and wit, not your pocketbook. If that's not good enough for her, then you may have your answer right away. It's not a bad thing for a woman to enjoy being treated well. It is a bad thing to demand a level of extravagance that can't be afforded. If you present to her like this is something you can regularly do, then you have set the expectation, not her.

The other reason I say a restaurant instead of "coffee" or a "walk in the park" or even a concert or movie is that the purpose of dating someone new is to get to know them on a more substantive level. Coffee or a walk in the park might sound ideal for this, but it also gives the impression that you are not serious or are hedging your bets. You get coffee with a friend or business associate. You walk in the park with someone you are already in a relationship with. Likewise, going to an event that doesn't afford you the chance to really talk about anything defeats the purpose of the "getting to know you" phase of dating.

So, pick a setting that affords you the ability to talk but also demonstrates a commitment beyond a simple conversation at a coffee shop.

The conversation should really be about getting to know appropriate but informative things like where they are from, family, what they do or hope to do, and what they are studying.

Be ready to get the conversation going with questions, and to keep it moving with questions!

Good example: "So where did you grow up? . . . Oh, Los Angeles, I've visited once but never had a chance to really explore. What was it like growing up there?"

Bad example: "Where are you from? . . . Oh, Los Angeles, that sucks, the traffic is horrible."

"Where are you from?" is too general. "Where did you grow up?" is more specific.

Showing interest in where someone grew up invites them to tell you more about what they liked or didn't like about it, which is insight into core memories and experiences. What they did, with whom, and why it was meaningful to them all paint a picture of the things that mean something to that person and inevitably helped shape them.

Ask questions that demonstrate you are paying attention and are interested but aren't inappropriately invasive.

For instance, if she refuses to bring up family, or does so in a way that suggests there's an estranged relationship, don't ask her to dig into that. If she wants to, that's one thing, but don't pry.

Women will often give you the key to having a good conversation with them if you really listen to them.

OTHER FACTORS:

1. **Transportation:** Once upon a time, I might have said, ensure that you pick her up, but again, you ignored me

and didn't really know this person, so getting her address and having her ride home be dependent upon you is probably not the best play. Be open if she asks for it, but don't make her feel obligated. You can get her a cab.

2. **Dress:** Put some effort into your appearance. Hygiene is incredibly important to women for a variety of very good reasons. I have a chapter on how to look good, but for a date, it should be like the restaurant: go as high-end as you can maintain.

SCENARIO 2: FIRST DATE WITH SOMEONE YOU ARE VERY FAMILIAR WITH

A first date with someone you already know and have greater knowledge of is infinitely better in MOST ways. The one way it isn't is that a friendship can be strained if the possible romance doesn't work out.

How do you set up a first date with someone you have probably obviously been attracted to and who has probably wondered when you would finally work up the courage to ask them out?

Let's start off with some assumptions. You already know each other's core values, a little bit of family history, and have a reasonably good idea of what the other one wants out of life, with respect to whether they want a family, have defined career goals, and so on.

So operating off said assumption, let's break this down.

First of all, don't go too romantic. Yes, the same rule applies as with someone you don't know very well. The reason for this is that while you may know this person better, you haven't been romantic yet. This is your first foray, and you don't need to scare the poor woman.

That means you can be more thoughtful in what you do. While the range of possibilities with a veritable stranger is isolated to environments where she can feel safe enough to open up, a first date with someone you know can feature more thought.

This is also where grabbing coffee together or going to a place of mutual interest, like a park, museum, and so on, can be an acceptable date to determine whether you both feel like pursuing something more.

LESSON 40

HOW TO DATE YOUR WIFE

Dating your wife can be harder than you think. Especially once you start having kids.

This is another reason that having close friends and family is important. They can watch the kids for you, because you really need to try dating your wife. And I say this as someone who still needs to get better at this.

First, let's acknowledge, just like we have in other cases, that while there are some general principles that may apply to "most women," you're not married to "most women." You're married to a very specific woman. Hopefully, you have the ability—because you have the requirement—to customize here a bit. Let me give you an example of a time I got it right.

My wife has a rule when it comes to surprises. You can surprise her with gifts anytime. You can surprise her with events some of the time. You can surprise her with people NONE of the time (unless it is very close family or friends).

Armed with this knowledge, I went about setting up a surprise event date.

1. **Appropriate dress:** Guys, let me tell you something, I don't care how great the event, concert, movie, play, whatever else it might be is, if you have not created the conditions where she is dressed for the occasion, she is going to spend half the night worrying about it. So, ensure that you have considered this.

2. **What to do with the kids:** If you have kids, especially kids who can't care for themselves, you have to be the one to make arrangements to have them watched. And it can't just be with anyone. It has to be someone SHE trusts, otherwise she will spend half the night worrying about the kids.

3. **Her interest, not yours:** Look, it's ideal if you both enjoy the event, but it's essential that she does, otherwise the odds of her sleeping with you later decrease greatly, and while that shouldn't be the point of setting up this date for your wife, we all know it would be totally cool with you if it ended that way!

4. **Your wife specifics:** This is all the stuff you have to account for concerning your wife. Diet, preferences, hang-ups, allergies, that thing Susan said that she is still irritated about, cycle (if she needs to bring things with her), and so on. It is easy for guys to blow stuff off in this category, but remembering the small stuff is not just a convenience; it tells her that not only do you listen to her but you "hear her." Which is to say, you listened with the intent of understanding AND remembering AND applying! The trifecta!

Before I take a victory lap on this success, let me share with you a story when I did not get this right.

My wife and I did not have a honeymoon. We had a nice wedding and reception with friends and family, but the very next morning, I had to fly back to Fort Bragg because I was in the 82nd Airborne at the time, and we got block leave only twice a year. So, for our first anniversary, I decided to give us the honeymoon we never got.

My plan was a seven-day Caribbean cruise. But that's not what I told her. I told her we were going to Disney World. (It was much cheaper then.) It was foolproof: The drive to the port was fairly similar, so we would head down from North Carolina, she would fall asleep on the drive, and when she woke up, we would be in front of a cruise ship instead of at Disney, and she would be so excited.

Now, keep something in mind: At this point in our marriage, I was a private first class in the Army, and she was working for Clinique at Belk, which was a department store. As you can imagine, I wasn't booking Royal Caribbean. We now affectionately refer to it as "Bob's Cruise Line" because I can't even remember the name of what it actually was. It doesn't really matter because it went out of business less than a year after our cruise, if I remember right. But hey, for a young married couple in their early twenties, it was awesome, and neither of us knew any better.

As we get closer to the date, my beautiful bride keeps asking me all of these "ridiculous" questions like "Where are we staying?" "How much is it?" "What do I need to budget for food?" "Did you already get the tickets?" and other such probing nonsense, which I of course answered with the super-assuring "Babe, I got this, don't worry." Now, keep in mind, she was the one handling the budget at that time and knew very well we had no money. So, how exactly I planned to pull off this Disney trip was a bit of an understandable mystery, which, surprisingly enough to my twenty-year-old self, was not solved by me just saying, "Babe, I got this."

Anyway, it got so bad that the night before we were supposed to leave, she got frustrated (which I now understand, but did not at the time). We were arguing about what the plan was and if we could actually afford any of this, and she finally just said, "You know what, I don't think you really have any idea of what is going on, and I don't even want to go."

Oh really!? Well, I did what all mature twenty-year-old husbands do. I left our crappy apartment in a sketchy area of town, and I went to the grocery store and bought flowers. I then came home and told her to sit down because she was about to feel "really bad." I explained that we weren't actually going to Disney but that I had planned a seven-day Caribbean cruise and that it was all taken care of, and I wanted it to be a surprise, but little Miss Grand Inquisitor wouldn't let me, so there.

She did feel bad. And we then were happy, and we had a great time. Except for when the black pearl necklace I got her in St. Thomas was stolen, but that's a different story for another time.

Now you may be thinking that I was the good guy in all of this, and for some time, I thought I was as well. And while I certainly intended to do something nice, I made the mistake of thinking I could just "surprise" my wife without taking into account how my setup for that surprise was causing a lot of unnecessary and understandable stress. But I learned.

So, having learned from my previous foray into surprises, I decided that this time, I would do it right. Here is the much more seasoned husband's approach to surprising my wife with a date.

My mission: Take her to dinner, *The Phantom of the Opera*, drinks, and then hotel and back home the next morning. I wanted to plan this surprise date in a way that would keep the surprise intact until the very last moment. Plus, in this case, it was an overnight stay, so I had to make sure a day bag was ready without her knowing, and be prepared to explain how all of the things that were going to instantly pop in her head were already taken care of—kids, dogs, day bag, and so on.

So, what did I do to account for these things?

Step 1 was telling her that we had to go to a formal work party, near the Kennedy Center, where *Phantom* was playing. I described the required dress and told her some of the people who would be there so that she had an idea of what to wear. Guys, this is important because even when we think we have given specifics on the official dress code, letting her know who will be there gives her a different level of indication of what to expect. I also told her what I was going to wear. This took care of the appropriate dress. She had a very good idea of what to wear, and I knew that if she felt comfortable going to the event I told her about, that same outfit would work for the play.

Step 2 was dealing with kids. At the time, my oldest daughter was old enough to watch the two younger ones overnight, plus our good friends lived less than two miles away. I made sure my oldest daughter had everything she needed and set it up with our friends to be able to check in. I also ensured that our daughter had a phone, knowing that no amount of preparation could prevent my wife from checking, so I made it a priority to make sure that my daughter was ready to answer immediately.

Step 3 of making it about her was easy, because my wife loves *The Phantom of the Opera*, and even though both of us had been, we had never been together. This was an opportunity not only to do something we both enjoyed but also to create a memory we could share together. And you better believe I told her just that!

Step 4 was all about ensuring that my wife's particular needs were met, not only through meticulous preparation but also by anticipating questions and being able to answer them immediately and with confidence. No "don't worry, babe, I got this" with Tina, because she knows I am the more spontaneous one and will sometimes fly by the seat of my pants. For her to have a good time with something I planned, I had to let her know everything was taken care of.

So, how did I break it to her?

Well, it was an hour and a half drive to the "event," and right before we got close to the place where I would have to turn to go a different direction, I asked her to reach into the glove compartment to get the tickets and make sure we had the address right. She pulled out the envelope and then looked at me and asked, "Are we going to *Phantom of the Opera*!?"

I smiled and said, Yes, babe, no work event, we are going to dinner, then *Phantom*. Then I have a place picked out for drinks or dessert afterward, and we are staying in DC tonight. The kids are in on it, and the Clancys know and are checking in on the kids. We will get back home late tomorrow morning. Everything is taken care of.

Boom baby, surprise achieved, excitement level achieved, confidence that kids, dogs, and logistics are taken care of achieved. We had a great time.

Now, not every date night needs to be an elaborate production. In fact, most of them don't need to be much more than dedicated time with the two of you getting to do something that allows you to focus on something other than the day-to-day activities of marriage or raising a family. Not that there is anything wrong with those things. But you can't complain about the romance or magic being gone from a marriage if you're not investing time in it.

But the rules still apply. It can just be dinner and a movie ten minutes from your house, and these are still the issues that matter.

Of all the things I've written about in this book, this is probably the one I am most guilty of, because it is difficult to maintain at times. Part of being married is being able to depend on someone when things get rough, hectic, or stressful, but that can't be the whole marriage.

So, guys, make the effort.

LESSON 41

HOW TO DEFEND THE SECOND AMENDMENT

1. Ensure people know what the 2A actually says.

2. Discuss why it was put there in the first place. (Hint: It wasn't hunting.)

3. Explain that infringing on the rights of all because of the actions of a few is a dubious way to protect a free society.

"The Second Amendment was meant for muskets!"

Okay then, was the First Amendment only for quill pens? See how ridiculous that sounds? I once got into something of a spat online when I responded to a TikTok "civics teacher" elaborating on why she didn't think we should be allowed to own AR-15s.

The premise of her argument was that the word *AR-15* doesn't appear anywhere in the Constitution, so this gun must not be included.

She therefore dared us to show her where in the Constitution you had a right to have an AR-15, because she was, in her words, a "whole ass civics teacher."

I explained that the AR-15 wasn't in the Constitution because it hadn't been invented yet. Just like the First Amendment doesn't mention email or specific religions or specific newspapers. The reason for this is that the founders used general language to describe the categories they were protecting from government interference. It would have been a fairly lengthy document had the founders listed every single medium of verbal or written exchange that existed or could ever exist, in order for it to be protected under the First Amendment.

I would have thought this was obvious, or at least it should have been to a "whole ass civics teacher." But apparently not.

Arguments like these are the veritable zombies of the antigun movement. No matter how many times they are killed, they return.

This is probably because they have the benefit of being superficially plausible to anyone who is "concerned" but not very well "informed." These kinds of arguments can be highly effective to anyone unaware of the purpose of the Second Amendment, unable to apply critical thinking, or driven by an emotional urge to "do something" the moment something bad happens with a private citizen and a gun. And chances are, if a child attends public school, this is exactly the kind of "informed citizen" that is being created by this kind of "whole ass civics teacher."

Let's look at what the amendment actually says: "A well-regulated militia, being necessary to the security of a free state, the right of the people to keep and bear arms shall not be infringed."

You will notice that there is nothing in there about "hunting" or "sport shooting." That's because the founders didn't write it out of fear that the deer may one day rise up against us.

The reality is that the Second Amendment and gun rights in general are not about collecting, hunting, sport shooting, or anything else of that nature. Gun rights are about defense from aggression, whether that aggression comes from a foreign invader, a criminal, or your own government.

Let's look at these reasons individually.

A Foreign Invader: Those who favor greater restrictions on private gun ownership will often refer to the first portion of the Second Amendment and offer it as evidence that what the founders really intended was for a "well-regulated militia" to have the ability to keep and bear arms, and since that role is now fulfilled by the National Guard, those are the only people who have a "Constitutional right" to keep and bear arms.

Now, understand that while the modern National Guard does bear resemblance to and certainly draws lineage from the original state militia system, it is a very different animal. State National Guards answer to the governor, until the president federalizes them. And since the vast majority of funding for guard units comes from the federal government instead of the states, it's not hard to see how the National Guard is effectively just another element of the national military instead of a state militia in the original sense.

At the Virginia Ratifying Convention, George Mason famously said, "I ask, Sir, what is the militia? It is the whole people." The founders saw every American as responsible for protecting our land and liberty against invaders.

The founders were skeptical of standing armies, and especially skeptical of armies being exclusively in the hands of federal authorities.

Historically, militias were made up of all able-bodied men within a particular community, who could be called upon in times of danger or crisis to provide security for their area. They were predominately defensive in nature but could engage in offensive operations. The term *well-regulated* at the time of its enshrinement in the Constitution was more akin to *well disciplined*. Militias were also made up of citizens who were responsible for bringing their own weapons with them. As dispersed regions merged into larger, politically designated areas or officially recognized states, they formed state militias to facilitate greater coordination and cooperation.

The creation of a federal government was never meant to completely take over the role of "securing a free state"; rather, its task was to create armies and navies while providing a coordinating function between the state militias. Take, for instance, the US Civil War.

At the outbreak of the Civil War, the United States Army and Navy were incredibly small, with many of our forces being dedicated to frontier service and our naval operations designed to protect shipping lanes and harbors, and defend against piracy. When troops were needed, the federal government did not rapidly expand the size of active-duty units within the standing federal army. They relied on the states to raise militias. The South actually did the same.

The Federal Army of the Potomac was composed of units like the 20th Maine, 1st Pennsylvania Cavalry, 69th New York Infantry, and so on. Likewise, Confederate forces included the 9th Virginia Infantry, 3rd Georgia Infantry, 1st Tennessee Cavalry, and so on.

The state militia system was designed to be composed of private citizens who could be called up for both federal service and domestic insurrection and tumults. The private ownership of firearms was a key component of that system.

But the original purpose was not simply to "fight wars" but to "secure a free state." And whether the departure from state militias has achieved that objective remains to be seen.

So the question to ask your opponent is, if some terrorist group tried to commit an October 7–style attack, do you want your town to be ready? The founders did.

Self-Defense or Protection from Criminals: Support for gun rights tends to grow the farther you get from the nearest police station.

The second half of the Second Amendment says "the right of the people to keep and bear arms shall not be infringed." The Supreme Court has decided once and for all that it includes an individual right to keep and bear arms. The founders recognized that the ability to defend oneself and property was absolutely essential to maintaining a free society. A "free society" is ultimately determined not by the ability of the government to protect its interests but by the ability of the people to protect theirs.

A citizen who is completely dependent upon a government entity for protection is one who will inevitably be left at the mercy of criminal elements, for the simple reason that law enforcement cannot be everywhere at once. Most people are shocked to learn that their law enforcement agencies have no legal obligation to protect them. This is not some kind of gross oversight or nefarious plot; it is a simple practicality. While the "intention" of law enforcement may be to protect people and their property, it cannot be a legal obligation; otherwise, every time a crime takes place, victims would be able to sue the government for failing to protect them.

Instead, law enforcement is legally obligated to "enforce the law." That includes the pursuit, investigation, trial, and punishment of lawbreakers for the purpose of punishment, prevention, safety, and restitution. And while all of those things may be noble pursuits, and worthy of support, they won't do you a lot of good AS you're being mugged.

And yet people will insist that you don't need a gun because we have law enforcement. One of the most pernicious implications of the "that's why we have the cops" argument is that it often implies that we bear no responsibility for our own security, which can be a breeding ground for foolish behavior. But more than that, it conflates "security" in general with the obligation to "secure a free state." While I agree that law enforcement can play an important role in securing a free state, the police can't be exclusively responsible for it.

So, we must ask ourselves an important question. If the government is not under any legal obligation to protect you from crime, is it reasonable to allow that same government to deprive you of the basic tools necessary to protect yourself?

The question to ask your opponent is, if you're alone in a cabin in the woods near a prison and known for bears, do you want to have no gun? The founders wanted you to have one.

Protection from Your Own Government: That last reason seems to be the one that concerns people the most.

"You really think you can take on the US military with pistols and rifles and win?"

Checking in with the founders . . . yup, turns out they beat the most powerful army in the world at the time, relying largely on militias and an underfunded and ill-equipped Continental Army.

"I'm not talking about 250 years ago when everyone had flintlock muskets. I'm talking about modern jet fighters up against guys with an AR-15."

Checking with the Taliban real quick . . . yup. Turns out that's possible too.

But here's the reality: Individual gun ownership is essential to the security of a free state. A genuinely free state is not one where you get to vote. It's one where you have a mechanism in place to fight back against an oppressive government.

The very ability to resist is sufficient to make overzealous politicians and government officials think twice about what they propose to implement. That's right, the right to keep and bear arms, by its simple existence, can serve as a healthy deterrent for would-be tyrants of any stripe.

The question you should ask your opponent is, do you think it would be possible for an armed populace to stop authoritarian actions in a city in your state? The founders wanted them to be able to try.

LESSON 42

HOW TO PREPARE YOUR KIDS FOR THEIR FIRST JOB

1. Reinforce the right mindset to avoid entitlement.

2. Give your kids jobs and responsibilities early on and hold them accountable for performance.

3. Encourage them to be creative and innovative in their problem-solving.

4. Explain the difference between doing a job and owning the job.

A common refrain among employers is that many younger job applicants seem to be wholly unprepared to take on even the most basic of responsibilities. And that includes preparing for the interview.

Some of this may be the "kids these days" syndrome that every older generation seems to catch once they get into their mid-forties, but there does seem to be something to this. Chalk it up to social media, Hollywood, schools, or whatever else you like; I'm sure you will find relevant examples and possibly some areas that need drastic improvement. Ultimately, the responsibility lies with you as the parent. Here are some ways to ensure that your kids aren't included in one of the "kids these days" stories.

Create the right mindset. While religious mores, societal norms, legal codes, and even observable nature suggest that children are owed protection and provision from their parents, children still need to be grateful for it. In a world where everyone talks about "rights" devoid of responsibilities, people seem to think that the right to "pursue happiness" is synonymous with having "happiness provided for you." That is a horrible mindset. It's natural for parents to want to provide for their kids, or even "give them the things you never had." But as I once heard Dennis Prager put it: "While you're busy giving your kids what you never had, don't forget to give them what you did have." That includes a sense of resilience, perseverance, gratitude, and a duty to contribute. Believing that you are "entitled" to something you haven't worked for is corrosive not only for the individual but for society. Instill in your kids early on that they need to produce, not just consume.

Give your kids "unpaid" jobs around the home early on. I put "unpaid" in quotes because while it may be unpaid, it is not uncompensated. Yes, you have an obligation to care for your children, but teaching them the importance of contributing to what they are getting is an important lesson. That's how life works.

Encourage them to admire entrepreneurship and good management. This is sorely lacking in the education system and even demonized in their cartoons. It's always the "greedy businessman" or "developer" who is going to destroy the nice park if kids with their kitten, dog, or backpack don't intervene. The employer is always the bad guy while the employee is often portrayed as the put-upon "wage slave" just trying to take care of their sick grandma in a capitalist wasteland. What a load of crap. But if you want your kids to know it's a load of crap, then take them through the process of putting together a small venture. It could be a lemonade stand, or in the case of my kids, it was selling jewelry or even making balloon animals at street festivals when they were young. Watch them go through the process of assessing a need in the marketplace, spending money up front on the capital or skills to meet that need, investing hours getting inventory together or anticipating levels of demand, and after all their work pays off, inform them that all they did was put some beads on a piece of string or blow up some ballons in funny shapes, and now you need 20 percent of what they made in taxes." I promise you they will not look kindly on the complete disregard of all their efforts or the confiscation of what they earned . . . not to mention the risk they assumed! And all of this is without employees to take care of. Trust me, they will have a new appreciation for what it means to run a successful business.

Emphasize capabilities, not just credentials. This is true of their overall economic well-being, not just their first job. Too many kids these days actually believe that if they get a degree, they are automatically entitled to a six-figure salary. And it's hard to blame some of them, since politicians and universities have been pushing it. The reality is that a credential can be incredibly beneficial, especially for securing an opportunity, but it doesn't guarantee that you will keep your job. That is, while a credential may be necessary to get the job, it will almost never help you keep it. Capabilities, especially those in high demand, are what help you keep a job or build and expand your business. Always encourage your kids to be constantly developing and mastering marketable capabilities; that way, they are never dependent upon just one skill to feed themselves. It also changes their mindset by getting them excited about the possibilities that come with capabilities.

Explain what working for someone else actually means.
When my oldest daughter got her first job at a local coffee shop owned by a friend of ours, I had two conversations. One with my daughter Lilly and one with our friend Brittney. I told Lilly that we were proud of her for getting a job and that we had complete confidence that she would be a responsible employee. I also told her that she needed to understand something about the nature of the arrangement that she was entering into. She was going to be paid to do a job, but the job itself did not "belong" to her. The job belonged to the person who created the opportunity, Brittney. What belonged to Lilly was her talent, work ethic, personality, and all the other attributes she was bringing to the job. Brittney had the right to find the best person for the job at the best price. Lilly had the right to seek the most money she could get for the work to be performed. Both of them had to agree, which meant that both of them had power. But once the agreement was made, it was time for both people to live up to their obligations to the other in this voluntary and mutually beneficial transaction.

I called Brittney and said, "We really appreciate you

hiring Lilly, and we are confident she will do a good job, but just so you know, we know how hard you worked to build this, so if you end up having to fire her because it isn't working out, you will get no grief from us."

I'm happy to report that not only did Lilly have a good experience, but so did our younger daughter, Ally. It was a great first job for both of them. That doesn't mean everything was perfect or there wasn't frustration at times; that is just part of life, but I am convinced that because our kids went into their first jobs with the correct mindset, they saw it as an opportunity, not an entitlement.

They also saw working for other people, especially small business owners, as an opportunity to learn more about entrepreneurship, because let's face it, in an ever-changing economy, the prospect of staying at the same job for twenty-plus years and retiring is getting slimmer. So, equip your kids to see opportunities where other people see only problems. And then encourage and facilitate the development of those marketable capabilities that will equip them to adapt, innovate, and overcome, as opposed to the entitlement mindset that seems to be dominating these days.

LESSON 43

HOW TO ARGUE IN FRONT OF YOUR KIDS

Your kids don't need to see you argue, but they need to see you work toward a resolution.

Yes, there are certain discussions where you need to dismiss your children from the room or remove yourself from a situation to have the argument in private. But if you can have the argument in front of your kids, there are reasons why you should.

My wife and I argue. Passionately from time to time. This is a very natural by-product of the fact that we are both opinionated and passionate people. We discuss weighty topics of religion, politics, situational ethics, possible scenarios, and numerous other topics that are likely to create some form of disagreement, if not in fundamentals, then of strategy or approach. Because my wife and I share the same values and faith, almost all our arguments are focused on how to achieve a common goal rather than the goals themselves. This is important. We are dedicated to one another, and our objective, as mentioned before, is to come to an agreement, not "defeat the other."

Let me share a story. My wife and I were arguing about a topic. I can't even remember what it was, but both of us were taking turns making our points, and both of us were pretty sure that we were right. About five minutes into the argument, a friend started getting nervous, basically trying to get us to "calm down" and trying to change the subject. But Tina and I were calm. We weren't yelling at one another or disparaging each other; we were just passionately discussing a matter of importance. And keep in mind, it's not as if this were a special event where we were disturbing or distracting others; we were in our own home and just discussing an issue, so what was the problem?

Well, it probably had something to do with the relationships this friend had had. In her experience, arguing meant something was fundamentally wrong with the relationship. There were very few topics that could be passionately discussed because they always led to deeper, underlying problems in the marriage. Arguments equaled divorce. So, it isn't hard to understand why having a spirited discussion could trigger bad memories and signify for her something that never occurred to Tina or me.

After all, for us, this was actually kind of fun. We enjoy challenging one another on weighty issues. We enjoy spirited debate.

But having said that, why do I suggest having such discussions about important issues in front of your kids? A few reasons.

The first has to do with their well-being. I know that probably sounds counterintuitive, because why would parents arguing be healthy for children? Because when arguments are respectful, productive, and, perhaps most important, successfully resolved, your children learn that they aren't a problem when done right.

Your children also see that Mom and Dad are strong in their relationship. Challenges aren't things to be swept under the rug, ignored, or dismissed, but something to be worked through together.

Lastly, and this is where the respect comes in, your children are learning how a husband and wife should resolve differences in opinion in order to get to common ground.

I want my children not only to have the courage of their convictions but also to be able to think about and discuss them intelligently. Observing Tina and me debate an issue shows them that this is a normal part of a healthy and loving relationship when done correctly.

So, what does a healthy argument look like?

1. **Purpose:** Reiterate that the goal is to ultimately arrive at the same conclusion, if at all possible, not to defeat one another in an argument.

2. **Respect:** While an argument is hardly likely to be completely devoid of emotion or sarcasm, you should always avoid yelling or condescension.

3. **Remaining constructive:** This is about effective problem-solving, not scoring points.

4. **Reconciliation:** Making sure everyone knows that the parents are good. Mommy and Daddy are passionate and sometimes disagree, but are always ultimately on the same side.

LESSON 44

HOW TO PROTECT YOUR KIDS FROM WOKE NONSENSE

If you teach your kids how to reason, how to find meaning, and you demonstrate these values in how you live your life, it's very hard to lose them to mindless ideology. When you see an angry, woke college student screaming at a protest, you might be seeing someone whose childhood left a hole so big only nonsense could fill it.

My oldest daughter is a theater kid. You would be hard-pressed to find a more "woke" environment than the theater. The arts in general have long been seen as a place to push boundaries and challenge the status quo. Sometimes for good, sometimes for ill. Lately it seems to be mostly for ill.

So, when my fourteen-year-old daughter announced that she really wanted to try out for a play at an all-boys school, I was cautious. The school advertised a lot of traditional values, and so one side of me thought that this might be the ideal place for her to be involved in theater. The girl-dad in me said . . . an "all-boys school"!?

But they regularly did casting calls for the female roles, and I thought hey, if they at least understand the value of having girls play the female roles, that's at least something.

Her first time out, she got a leading role in the play *Guys and Dolls* as Sarah Brown. So, my daughter got the part of a prim, proper, and pious missionary named "Sergeant Sister Brown" . . . awesome. Who falls in love with a gambler who flies her to Cuba for lunch . . . wait, what the hell!?

In a funny turn of events, her love interest in the play was four years older and just so happened to be the son of my chief of staff and dear family friend.

But that also means she falls in love with an older boy and has several scenes where they are supposed to kiss. I'm now hating this idea.

The first thing she made very clear to the director was that she was kissing no one. She was fine with a "stage kiss" where you maneuver yourself in such a way that it looks like you're getting kissed, but you aren't. She was not, under any circumstances, kissing anyone. She was very polite about it and recognized that if that meant she couldn't have the part, she would understand, but she was firm. The director liked her so much, he accommodated the request.

She did an outstanding job and went on to be in several more plays with the school. Her younger sister even joined in and was in a few herself. They both had a great time, and it was a wonderful experience for them. Throughout the years both of my daughters have had to address intellectual and social challenges in that environment. They have handled them with grace and intelligence . . . although when it comes to debating her fellow theater kids, my youngest daughter may be a little more "facts don't care about your feelings" than my oldest . . . lol. So why do I mention all of this?

Many people believe that protecting your kids from "woke" means sheltering them. And in some ways, it is. But it's also about careful exposure. I am grateful that she had the opportunity to star in several plays with the school, but this does not mean she wasn't exposed to a wide array of ideas, concepts, and language that don't quite fit into our worldview.

The theater, even high school theater, likes to tackle the political issues of the day. The students all discuss these issues. She was starring in plays during BLM riots, Defund the Police, Donald Trump, COVID, Drag Queen Story Hour . . . you name it. It was as if every woke concept ever dreamed up was a debate on the twenty-four-hour news cycle right as my teenage daughter was going through some of her most formative years, spending her evenings as part of a theater group where all the ideas we taught her were being openly challenged by peers and authority figures.

So, how do you, as a parent, handle it?

By talking about it and not being afraid of it. That means discussing it, not dismissing it.

As a homeschool parent, people often assume that the way we maintain loyalty to our beliefs is through a complete lack of exposure to others. That is obviously not what we did.

I often tell people that as a parent, my job is to protect my kids from scars, not bruises. They are going to have to go out and try certain things, challenge things, and fail at times. That way, they can learn the value of not only getting back up but overcoming past failure in order to learn from it and move on to success.

The same is true of your belief system.

We didn't want our kids to simply regurgitate what we believed. We didn't want to simply set up an "authority structure" that they had to obey or else. We wanted them to believe that what we taught them was true. Ultimately, that is the only way the beliefs and ideas can become their own.

We started by teaching them what we believed and why. We then did our best to live up to it and admitted when we failed. We wouldn't allow them to simply regurgitate what we said; we challenged them to think about it and would argue the other side of the debate to them to see how they might respond and, in fact, to help them develop responses.

Clever questions were rewarded in our family and not punished. We would discuss issues from different angles and approaches, and perhaps one of the most important things we did was help our children separate beliefs from the person. We were adamant that there is such a thing as truth and right and wrong. But we also taught them that people are fallible, and that oftentimes there can be a lot of unspoken pain behind a very bad idea. So, try to understand why someone believes something, not necessarily so that you can adopt a bad idea or "let something go" to fit in or make someone feel better; it's so that you can better understand how to approach the topic for the person you are discussing it with.

While many kids are taught to avoid discussions on "politics or religion," we taught ours that these were some of the most intellectually stimulating, deepest, and richest conversations one could have. Like anything else, there was a place to give it a rest, but knowing what you believe and why about topics such as God, truth, morality, policy, freedom, and logic were concepts to embrace, not avoid out of a false sense of politeness. I have increasingly become convinced that parents have been encouraged to avoid discussions of "politics and religion" not so that the topics wouldn't be discussed but so that students would look everywhere but their parents to discuss them.

For instance, our daughters would come home from play practice eager to tell us not only about the interesting aspects of the character or script they had but also about the conversations they had had with directors and peers. They wanted to share the topics that came up, the arguments that were made, and how they responded to them. It all made for great opportunities for them to learn about different perspectives, but also challenge their own beliefs and the statements of others.

They quickly learned that they were prepared to understand

different perspectives and apply both logical and emotionally sensitive arguments in defense of what they believed, even to an audience that outnumbered them at best and was occasionally hostile from time to time. As their success in this environment grew, so did their confidence, not only in what they believed, but in their ability to present it well.

It was in that moment that we realized that the worldview we wished to pass on to our children had been accepted by them. Not because they could easily repeat back what they had been taught, but because they possessed both the capability and the desire to defend it before peers and authority figures they respected.

Here are ten things we learned by trying to protect our kids from woke madness.

1. Control what your children watch and are exposed to at a young age. Cable, smartphones, and social media can all wait until your children possess the appropriate amount of maturity. Handing your kid the internet is the same as handing your kid TO the internet.

2. Be aware of the relationships they are developing and the influences they have. This is much easier if you homeschool.

3. Don't be afraid to have strict rules about dating.

4. Be aware of the authority figures you trust to educate your children. Part of the problem with completely outsourcing education to anyone, but especially the government, is that your children no longer see you as someone to learn from. Because after all, you aren't an "expert" because you don't have a teaching degree.

5. Reward honesty. Especially when it comes at a cost. This doesn't mean that you forgo punishment when

necessary. Kids need to learn that doing the right thing sometimes includes pain. But give them respect for it, and you will be shocked at what they are willing to stand up for when you aren't around.

6. Know that the attitudes and behaviors they demonstrate in their teens began to be set when they were a toddler. If you let your kids get away with bad and disrespectful behavior when they are little because they are "just at that age," soon you will be excusing bad behavior because they are "just going through a phase," and before you know it, you have a little adult you don't even want to be around.

7. Admit when you are wrong to your kids, but only if you are actually wrong. Taking blame for something you shouldn't, just to maintain the peace, teaches your kids that manipulation is how they get their way.

8. Teaching your kids to think critically MUST be done by you. If you don't know how, learn. You would be shocked at how "logic" and "critical thinking" are taught at most institutions.

9. Conduct thought and scenario exercises with your kids. It not only engages them in thinking through difficult problems or situations but also teaches them to imagine and consider potential scenarios before they go into them. You're not just preparing them by doing this; you're teaching them to prepare themselves.

10. When you do have to deny them access to something, be it a party entertainment, the "freedom" to do something others are doing, or buying something everyone else

has, don't just tell them the dangers they are avoiding. Focus them on the advantages it will bring. Delayed gratification and good decision-making are keys to long-term success. You're not taking something away from them; you are preparing them to get something better.

I could have written another ten things about what I wished I had done better. And not every one of these ten is something we executed perfectly. I can't tell you how much I begged God that He would step in where I failed. The amazing thing about all this advice is how forgiving and resilient kids can be when you put in the effort, and they feel loved and safe with you.

I'm proud to say that my twenty-two-year-old, nineteen-year-old, and seventeen-year-old are all embracing the values we hoped they would and are capable of standing up for them.

There really is no greater sense of pride and relief than watching your children continue to build their relationship with God and look toward the future with confidence.

LESSON 45

HOW TO SHOW YOUR WIFE GRATITUDE

Being a military spouse is difficult without a war. But during wartime, it is especially difficult due to long periods of separation and the prospect of dying. For the first ten years Tina and I were married, I spent about half of it away. Everything from training, schools, deployments, and combat deployments—all meant that Tina found herself having to raise our kids without me there. Had she wanted to become bitter, I think most people would have understood. But she didn't.

That is not to say that there weren't times when we argued about it. But whenever I deployed, Tina took the attitude that all of us were serving. One person might deploy, but the whole family goes to war. She set about getting things in order, making sure she knew where to send mail, care packages, and so on. She would make the kids shirts and pillowcases with pictures of Daddy on them so that they could remember what I looked like and get the feeling that I was still with them, still watching over them, even though I was on the other side of the world.

When I would come home, she always made sure that I felt missed, loved, and honored for my service. My kids were always excited to see me because, despite the fact that it was incredibly hard on Tina, she constantly told my children that I was a hero, a warrior, defending our family and our country.

This made all the difference in the world. I can't tell you how much I appreciated it. Even more so when I heard stories of other homecomings, which bore no resemblance to mine. Animosity, frustration, affairs, and sometimes divorce papers.

Gentlemen, when you marry for values, before anything else, there is a great chance that you will be with someone you can weather any storm with and come out better on the other side. But that effort has to be reciprocated. I could write an entire book on things I have gotten wrong in my marriage or could have done better, but I can tell you that I never took for granted the incredible role my wife played during that difficult time. To this day, I can't speak of it without getting choked up for the gratitude I feel.

> Men, make sure your wife feels gratitude for the things she does and the sacrifices she makes to help build up your family. Show it in your actions, but verbalize it as well. Maybe it isn't war for you, maybe it's something else that she has to overcome in order to support the role you play, but whatever it is, recognize it when it happens. Express that you appreciate how hard it must have been and how proud and blessed you are to have her. She doesn't just need to hear it; she deserves to.

LESSON 46

HOW TO KNOW WHAT YOU ARE WILLING TO DIE FOR

Do you follow Christ? Are you married? Are you a father? Are people depending on you in a dangerous situation? Then you should know what you are willing to die for.

Allow me to explain.

It's interesting what you think about when you're pretty sure you're about to get shot. It wasn't the first time it was a very real possibility; I just had never had this much time to think about it. Every other time I was in a stack, lined up on a door with other Green Berets, or Iraqi scouts, it was all pretty straightforward. You jumped off the vehicles, ran to your entry point, stacked on the door, and bang . . . kick it in and start flowing through the house. Room to room, house to house, speed and violence of action to maintain momentum and surprise anyone who might have been inclined to run or fight.

This time was different.

We had gone to this little house next to the Tigris River not to hit a target but to speak with the owner. We had just come from a different target where we had rolled up someone who was supposed to be a lieutenant in a local terror cell, but the second stop was just to gain information. I was the senior NCO on the objective, and I accompanied the Iraqi major I was advising into the house where he planned to discuss a particular terror cell leader we knew who used to bed down in the vicinity. As the major walked into the other room, an explosion went off outside.

I threw my helmet back on and ran out the door to see an Iraqi running past me. There were about forty-five of us on the objective: five Green Berets, about twenty-five Iraqi Army, and another fifteen or so militia who didn't always have recognizable uniforms. I yelled at the running Iraqi, and he shouted "Sahwa" to let me know he was militia. I told him he was running in the wrong direction and proceeded to move toward the sound of gunfire next to the river.

We had two wounded, and every Iraqi with a gun was firing in what we affectionately called the "Jundi Death Star," *jundi* being the Arabic word for a private. I started to see the other guys from the team come online, ensuring that all our Iraqi scouts and militia were at the very least firing in the right direction as we attempted to get our wounded to safety and set up a perimeter to ensure that whoever had started the fight didn't get away.

Before I go on, you need to understand something about this part of Iraq. Away from the river, it looks like flat desert. Visibility is pretty good. Next to the river, it gets lush and thick. We weren't more than thirty meters from the river, and you couldn't see it in the backyard of this house for all the trees and tall grass.

We started to take the Iraqis and clear any structures to the left and right of where the explosion had taken place. The most important thing was to ensure that we established a tight perimeter around the location. Our Communications SGT Chris already had Apache helicopter gunships patrolling up and down the Tigris to make sure no one got out. We were fairly quick to lock down the flanks, finding locations with a clear line of visibility toward the river on either side.

I remember feeling a sense of pride at how quickly the other guys on the team got right to where they needed to be, got everyone online, and set up a perimeter with very little instruction needed. Having worked together for some time now, everyone was capable of sizing up the situation and filling their role based on where they were when the fighting started. What started out as chaos had been returned to order in minutes.

There was only one problem. Where was the bad guy?

We had cleared everything so fast, had helicopters patrolling the area, that he didn't get across the river, and he couldn't have gotten past us. I was pissed. It seemed like we had moved quickly, but if he knew the area better than us, he could have gotten out. What if, seeing the militia, he simply walked past one of us with an AK-47 and blended in? I was walking down the perimeter line, getting more and more frustrated at the thought of this guy getting away, when I saw it.

It wasn't much. Just a portion of the grass that bent in the same direction, leading to the river. I got on the radio to Riley and let him know that I was going forward of the line with a militiaman and one of our interpreters. Whatever happens, tell the Iraqis not to fire. We slowly started following the trail, looking down at the grass and up ahead into a wall of tall grass and trees that we knew dipped down toward the Tigris just fifteen to twenty meters ahead of us. Then all of a sudden, the trail became a little more pronounced and dropped off into what looked like a hole leading to an underground bunker or hiding spot. I could see the water of the Tigris now, but I took out a flash-bang, a flashlight, and my M9 pistol. I tossed the flash-bang in, and as soon as it went off, I dove in with my pistol and flashlight.

The hiding spot was bigger than it looked from the outside and was obviously constructed. This had to have been where he was hiding, but no one was there.

Had anyone been there? I crawled back out of the hole and rejoined my interpreter and militiaman on the trail, incredibly frustrated.

What if the original explosion had been a booby trap? What if there hadn't been any bad guy to chase down? I had never seen anyone shooting back at us; there was only the one explosion, and while some of the Iraqis had sworn that they saw someone, and there was a lot of fire coming from our side, it was hard to tell if they had positively identified someone or if in the confusion of the explosion and everyone firing, they had simply imagined it.

We began to strongly consider that this had all been an IED, followed up by nervous militiamen firing into the trees and grass at an enemy they only imagined was there. And then we saw another portion of the trail, going in the opposite direction along the riverbank, and this time, looking down a steep slope, I could see blankets and other objects, which made it clear that this was a bed-down site. I remember telling my interpreter to yell at whoever was there to show me their hands.

No answer.

I pulled out another flash-bang and my pistol again, because my rifle would have been too difficult to maneuver in the narrow space I was about to jump into. My interpreter stopped me and told me to just "frag it." I thought about it for a second, but two things stopped me. Potential secondary explosions, and what if, after all this, there was some kid hiding down there?

Now this sucked.

There was clearly only one entrance into this space, and it had to be the last possible place this guy could be hiding, if there was anyone at all. And if he was down there, it's not like he was going to be surprised. If he's there, he's waiting, and he knows where I'm coming from. This was unlike any operation I had been on at this point. Every other time, we had chosen the time and place for the fight. Every other objective we hit hard and fast, offering our targets little to no time to respond. As a result, they took their chances with being captured rather than killed. But this guy, if there was a guy, had initiated contact. The odds of him throwing up his hands and quietly walking back to the truck were not good.

And that's when it hit me. There was a good chance that what I did next could decide whether I ever saw my family again.

And that's why it's interesting the things you think about when you think you're about to get shot. Or more specifically, get killed. Because no sooner had I run through the possible options in my head and the consequences of getting it wrong than I remembered a story my father had told me.

My father had been a homicide detective with the LAPD, serving on the officer-involved shooting team. In one instance, he was asked to investigate a shooting where two officers had been wounded and a suspect had been killed. The captain of the officers involved believed that his officer's decision to leave cover and rescue his partner while returning fire had been conducted outside policy and that the officer should be counseled and undergo additional training.

After reviewing the scene and circumstances, the review board brought in the officer and his captain and proceeded to congratulate the officer on his bravery and competence under fire. They told the captain that the review board would be looking on with extreme interest at what potential medal for heroism the captain would recommend for the officer he had essentially tried to throw under the bus.

Shortly after they dismissed the officer, my father and one of the other review board members found themselves on the same elevator as the captain. The captain looked over and asked, "You really don't think he was out of policy?" To which the other review board member said, "No, Captain, this is the job. We're the people they call. Unless, of course, you want people to start calling the fucking fire department."

We're the ones they call. My father had been the one they called. So had my grandfather. Now it was me. I looked up to the sky very briefly, prayed, and then . . . I figured it all came down to a pretty simple question. What can you live with? I could live with whatever happened next if I jumped in that hole. But I couldn't live with being a coward.

I pulled the pin on the flash-bang, tossed it in, and as soon as it went off, I jumped . . . because we are the ones they call.

LESSON 47

HOW TO KNOW WHEN IT'S *REALLY OKAY* TO CRY

"I want a man who's in touch with his feminine side."

No, she probably doesn't. And here is how you know. Every one of her guy friends who is super in touch with their "feminine side" is sitting securely in the friend zone, wondering when she will realize that he has always been there for her. You know . . . when she wanted to talk about how the guy she is actually dating doesn't understand her like "you do."

Now, before the ladies get mad at me, let me explain.

She does want you to demonstrate affection, tenderness, and even vulnerability with her when appropriate. But she only wants to know that you can do those things if she is also sure that you are brave, honest, capable, and able to handle yourself in high-pressure situations.

If you aren't the kind of guy capable of protecting her, then she is probably just not going to be as attracted to you, no matter how much "emotional intelligence" you possess. Hey, I didn't make up the rules. But if you think about this for a second, it makes sense.

Women are more physically vulnerable than men. This is why jobs associated with danger and physical labor are typically done by men. Women can get pregnant (yes, only women), and this represents an additional level of physical and emotional vulnerability. So, it is entirely natural for a woman to want a man who is capable of protecting and providing for her. These are basic, foundational-level requirements.

Does that mean she's lying when she says she wants a guy capable of being sensitive? Probably not. She just wants to make sure that the strong and capable man she's attracted to is also honest, loyal, and cares for her.

So how do you know when you can be emotionally vulnerable with a woman?

Rule 1: Be careful whom you trust with your emotions. Just like she has certain requirements of you when it comes to things like the ability to protect and provide, you get to have requirements of her when it comes to demonstrating emotional vulnerability. If she is the type of woman who laughs at or mocks you when you show vulnerability, she's not someone you should see anymore, and honestly, you shouldn't marry her.

Rule 2: Understand that men do display emotion. It just usually manifests itself in sarcasm and anger, because these emotions don't readily display weakness or vulnerability. Women will sometimes test a man to see if he's in control of his emotions, because let's face it, greater physical vulnerability means they should probably see if you're capable of controlling your emotions before they commit to you.

Rule 3: Know when it's okay to show vulnerability, but do it with a sense of decorum and strength: Yes, there are times when I cry or have a deeply emotional reaction to something. But I keep it together. You should never be so consumed or overwhelmed by your emotions that you lose control of yourself altogether. Again, your job is to represent stability and strength in the storm, and you can't do that if you're so overwhelmed by your emotions that you break down.

Rule 4: Emotion displayed by a strong man is far more valuable than emotion displayed by a weak one. The reason that a wife, son, or daughter will remember the time their strong father or husband cried is because he didn't do it very often. Not because he was emotionally unavailable, but because he was emotionally strong enough to be the rock for the family.

It's not that a real man never cries in front of others; he just never does so during crises.

If a close friend or loved one was to pass away suddenly, my first response is to think about what needs to be done to relieve the burden of those affected, to make the necessary arrangements, and to ensure that, in the midst of loss, people know that there is someone taking care of what needs to be done. To provide stability in the midst of uncertainty.

But once that is achieved, all that is left to be done is to honor and remember the person who passed. In that moment, they are worthy of that emotion.

LESSON

HOW TO ARGUE FOR PRO-LIFE

"It's just a clump of cells."

Okay, but then so are you.

If you had ever told me that 37 percent of the voting public was all for getting an abortion at any time and for any reason, all the way up to month nine, I probably would have said you were nuts. And yet here we are.

I know many men think that we should just sit this one out. I mean, after all, pregnancy affects women in ways it obviously doesn't affect men. And maybe there is something to that. I think all of us recognize that while anyone can speak on a topic or is entitled to their own opinion, we typically give deference to those individuals or groups most affected by a particular policy.

But if you're on the side of babies, you've almost certainly been a baby. That gives you some expertise in defending the right to allow babies to live.

Pro-choicers can't even be honest in who does and doesn't have a say, because the same people who will tell you that as a man you have no right to comment on abortion will praise men who "stand up" for women's "reproductive rights."

The abortion industry is telling you as a man to shut up, not because you shouldn't have an opinion, and certainly not because you don't have any influence on this issue. They are telling you to shut up because they know exactly how powerful you could be on this topic by the way you conduct yourself and by the strength you could bring to bear to save the innocent lives they have created an industry and culture around destroying.

So, let's go through the most common arguments for abortion and ask whether men can or should speak out on this topic.

1. **"It's not a baby, it's a fetus."** If you said, "It's not a toddler, it's an infant," can you kill the infant now? The fundamental question is not what stage of development the human life is at, but whether it is human life. If you believe in "human rights," then the question is at what stage of development do you meet all the reasonable criteria for being human and alive? At the point of conception, you meet the criteria we use to distinguish between life and nonlife, and you possess all the DNA code necessary to distinguish you not only from every other species of life but from every other human life. You're just at your earliest stage of development. So, this argument is ridiculous unless you believe that it's perfectly okay to arbitrarily kill innocent human beings, provided they are at a particular stage of life. In which case, you don't actually believe in "human rights."

2. **"Yeah, but it's not 'sentient' life."** Neither is a person in a coma. Does that mean it is okay to arbitrarily kill them?

3. **"It's about bodily autonomy."** Oh, I see, so does bodily autonomy apply as a general principle or just to certain people? Because if it is a general principle, and just about everyone who uses this argument believes it is a general principle, then why does it not apply to the fetus? "Well, because the fetus is using the woman's body against her will." I see, and how did the fetus get there in the first place? You see, the thing about bodily autonomy is it's a pro-life argument, not a pro-abortion argument.

4. **"The fetus is a parasite."** No, it literally isn't. Gosh, I love getting lectured about science by people who use this argument. The word *parasite* has a definition, and fetus doesn't fit into that categorization. A parasite is an organism that lives off its host, causing harm to the host. Can we please stop pretending that we don't know the difference between a fetus and a parasite?

5. **"This is about reproductive freedom."** No one is taking away your right to make decisions about when or with whom you would like to "reproduce." Just like no one is telling you how to earn a living. We are saying that if your "reproductive freedom" includes the arbitrary destruction of another human life, that is a problem. Just like me telling you that you can't rob convenience stores is not an infringement on your "occupational rights."

6. **"There are too many kids in poverty."** So your solution to kids in poverty is to kill kids in poverty? Do the kids in poverty get a say?

7. **"What if they have disabilities?"** Like Down syndrome? Trisomy 18? Physical deformities? The wrong color eyes?

What shall we classify as a deformity worthy of death? By the way, what kind of message does it send to all the children living with disabilities when they hear that your particular brand of compassion includes believing that they and the world would be better off without them?

We could go on, but I think you get the picture. This is about a fundamental principle of civilization that affects men differently from women, but it still affects us. Even if you could make a decent argument that it doesn't directly affect you in any way, why would that ultimately matter? The destruction of innocent human life is wrong. The brutal killing of the innocent is wrong.

I am a man. I am called to be a protector of the innocent. To use my strength to protect others. At the very least, that strength should be used to protect my children and the mother of my children.

One of the most important questions a mother ponders when choosing whether to get an abortion is whether the father will step up and support her. Be the kind of man she can depend on. Be the kind of man your child can depend on.

LESSON 49

HOW TO MAINTAIN CAPABILITIES INSTEAD OF JUST STORIES

1. Ranger School challenges you mentally and physically.

2. There are objective standards for success and failure.

3. You must innovate and adapt to both the environment and the people to achieve success.

4. It reminds me that there is a difference between "credentials" and capabilities. A credential tells people what you were able to do at one point. A capability is something you can still do.

Ranger School is arguably the greatest weight loss program in history, except for communism.

I went into Ranger School as an athletic paratrooper, weighing in at about 155 pounds. At that stage in my military career, I was twenty years old. I had been to Infantry Basic, Airborne, Air Assault, EMT, and Sniper School. I was in great shape with a metabolism that was rockin' it. And to be honest, I was a bit terrified. For your infantry soldier, Ranger School is the height of street cred. It's the premier light infantry school in small unit leadership and tactics. It's changed over time, but when I went through, it was about seventy days, if you didn't recycle. Not all that time was spent in the field, hungry, tired, and miserable, but enough of it was. To give you an idea, in those seventy days, I lost about 25 pounds, and at 155 and running five times a week, I didn't have 25 pounds of fat to lose. My wife later described seeing me as a bit shocking. Less like a graduation and more like being liberated from a camp. So, what did I learn?

Well, other than that sleep and food deprivation sucked, I learned a great deal about conducting ambushes, raids, and reconnaissance missions in difficult and varying terrain, under less-than-ideal conditions. Which sounds and is pretty cool. But one of the most important things I learned in Ranger School was what would happen to me when all typical motivation was gone and the only thing left was discipline and the fear of failure.

I managed to make it straight through without any recycles. The only close call was getting cellulitis in Mountain phase and having to get IV meds after finishing the patrol phase of Mountains, as we called it.

Graduating from Ranger School made me feel like a "made man." I remember how I felt as a young paratrooper when guys had "the tab." They were the experts, the badasses, the guys who could lead and do so under difficult circumstances. And now, at twenty-one, I was one of them. But was I?

I remember getting back to my scout platoon at the 82nd Airborne and going on our first "field problem"—a training exercise in the woods carrying out small-unit tactics against a mock enemy. My lieutenant and my platoon sergeant (both tabbed) looked at me and said, "Hey, Ranger, you plan the mission." No warning, no prep. They simply gave me the mission, the objective, and timelines, and expected me to develop and brief the operations order right there. The order includes the situation, mission, execution, service, communications, and support (think logistics plan, packing list, etc.). Execution means the whole plan for infiltration, actions on the objective, and exfiltration. I think they gave me a whole thirty minutes. Nothing I shouldn't be able to handle, right? I mean, after all, I was a Ranger-qualified paratrooper now, and that's what that tab meant . . . right?

I know it sounds stupid, but to my young, dumb self, that is where it first really sank in that the tab on my shoulder wasn't going to do the work for me. The tab was a symbol that I was the one who could do the work. It was not a symbol that I effectively did that job a few times in Ranger School. It was supposed to signify that I could do that job, and do it well, forever.

I remember rushing during those thirty minutes to put together the operations order and then briefed it with my leadership watching. I distinctly remember thinking "This sucks . . . I know I'm missing something. I probably screwed up something with the service and support paragraph. I hate freaking logistics. I'm about to get embarrassed and recognized for the fraud I am. Months of preparation and weeks of hating life in the woods and mountains of Georgia and the swamps of Florida to get my tab, and now I'm going to prove I just got lucky. DAMN IT!"

I finished briefing the plan. My lieutenant looked at my map and crudely thrown-together sand table (a visual depiction on the ground of how you plan to execute your actions on the objective). He said, "Looks good. Let's do it."

I pulled it off. I fooled them!

But I hadn't fooled them. I did know what I was doing. I may have still been dealing with the newness of it all, the inevitable feeling of imposter syndrome, but the fact was, I had "pulled it off" because the people who trained me had done a good job, and I had retained it.

Here is the bottom line. That day, I learned I was more capable than I thought I was. I still had a lot to learn. Tabs, medals, accomplishments, experiences: They are just cool stories of what once was, unless you insist on maintaining the capabilities they're supposed to represent.

A tab without a capability is the worst kind of window dressing. If you don't want the capability with the tab, you're looking for accolades, not prowess. And ultimately, you'll end up with neither.

> Looking back on one's accomplishments is not a bad thing. It means you've done something in your life. But look for ways to maintain, enhance, and increase the capabilities that made such accomplishments possible. Don't rest on your laurels; otherwise, you will find out all too late that you're not only no longer the man you were but not even the man you could be.

LESSON 50

HOW TO TEACH YOUR KIDS ABOUT "SHARING"

1. When sharing becomes mandatory, it's not sharing.

2. Telling your kids to "share" without context doesn't create generosity or altruism. It creates expectation and entitlement.

3. Sharing CAN be and often is a good thing, but it's not better than property rights. And in fact, sharing can exist only in a world WITH property rights.

4. No, I'm not being "too intense" here. Between participation trophies and demanding that everyone "share" by force, I think we've created the most self-absorbed and entitled people in history.

If you had asked me four years into being a parent what I thought about teaching my kids to share, I probably would have given you the typical "yeah, it's really important" speech. And it is. The problem is, like everyone else, I was doing it wrong.

Most parents have been encouraged to teach their kids not genuine "sharing" but something else entirely. And believe it or not, I think it has some pretty negative consequences.

Sharing, by definition, is voluntarily permitting someone else to use or consume your property. When my neighbor politely asks to borrow my gas-powered auger once, and I say yes, that's being a good neighbor. But is that what we are teaching?

I remember telling my kids to share their toys with their friends, without thinking much of it. Then one day, I saw a kid grasping at what other kids had while screaming "SHARE!!!" The moment he didn't get what he wanted, he ran to his parent, who promptly told the other child to "share." I realized something in that moment. We are teaching our kids two very bad lessons in the way we approach this seemingly simple concept.

1. We're teaching them that they can demand the use of someone else's property.

2. If the other person doesn't comply with that demand, the demander can run to an authority figure who will force you to let them have it.

And we wonder why so many young people think they have a right to other people's property. We wonder why college professors find it so easy to convince students that the forced confiscation and redistribution of other people's property is just. After all, if those with things we want won't "share," they should be forced to share, just like you were when you were a child.

Look, I understand that some people will read this and think I'm making a bigger deal out of this than I should, but we are only just now beginning to learn how children at a young age pick up on concepts and embed them into an understanding of the world.

My wife and I took this to heart and tried something different with our kids. We taught them that sharing was a decision they could make about their things. We taught them that there were basically two reasons to share. The first was charitable. It's nice to let someone use your property to bring them joy. The second is practical. Sharing can be a form of cooperation. It's an opportunity for both parties to expand their access to available resources through mutual benefit.

Now obviously we put this into kid language, which sounded a bit more like: "Your toys belong to you, and you don't have to share them, especially with someone who is being mean, but it can be a very nice thing to do! Plus, sharing also allows you and your friends to play with lots of toys, instead of you just playing with yours and them just playing with theirs."

Whenever our kids would say, "They're not sharing," we would respond, "Yeah, they don't have to. It's their toy and they don't owe you time to play with it." But then we would usually ask questions. Did you ask nicely? Did you offer to share your toys? Were they done playing with it?

All these questions reinforced a larger set of principles. Kindness, cooperation, boundaries, awareness, and yes, property rights, something that doesn't seem to be very respected these days.

Now here is the question. Did it work? My kids had no problem sharing, but they also didn't have a problem telling someone no. They were still required to do it politely and were reminded that others would treat them the way they treated others, but the decision was theirs.

I'm proud to report that this has caused all our kids to be generous with others, but our kids aren't pushovers. They have a general respect for other people's property, and perhaps most important, they don't feel a sense of entitlement about other people's stuff, nor do they feel a false sense of guilt over wanting to protect what they have earned.

LESSON

HOW TO ARGUE FOR FREE MARKET CAPITALISM

1. People have a right to own property that includes their labor.

2. People have a right to engage in voluntary trade.

3. People have a right to recompense from someone who damages, steals, or otherwise engages in coercive behavior to take their property.

4. Economic systems that respect the rights of people to own property and engage in trade are superior to those that use government force to restrict such actions.

5. Free market capitalism is the system that advocates for these principles and has not only achieved incredible material wealth within society but has allowed for the maximum freedom possible for people to choose how and when they

will interact with others in order to improve their own lives by providing goods and services that improve the lives of the people they are engaging in voluntary exchange with.

I'll never forget one day sitting in an English literature class in community college and being given *The Communist Manifesto* to read. Nothing screams "English literature" like the writings of a German communist.

The Communist Manifesto is perhaps the most famous of Karl Marx's writings on his political, economic, and social theories, which have become collectively known as "Marxism." Marx summarized his theory as the "abolition of the private ownership of the means of production." Interestingly enough, that description actually applies to both communism and socialism, which are nowhere near as different as modern-day socialists would like you to think. In fact, it could be argued that socialism is worse than Marxism, but that's a debate for another time.

So, we are given Marx to read, and the following week our professor asks us, "What do you guys think of capitalism?"

Think about that question for a moment. He didn't ask us what we thought of the prose or sentence structure. He didn't even ask us what we thought of communism. He asked us what we thought of capitalism. And keep something in mind, it's not as if the next book in our reading list was *Capitalism and Freedom*, by Milton Friedman, or *Economics in One Lesson*, by Henry Hazlitt. The only book we were given that featured any kind of economic treatise or argument, was written by the most famous opponent of free market capitalism to ever live, Karl Marx. And we were reading it not in an economics class but an English class, where the professor could be reasonably sure that none of the students would have anything remotely close to a firm understanding of economic theory. (And they certainly weren't going to learn any from *The Communist Manifesto*, which is more of a list of grievances than analysis.)

It should come as no surprise when the first student to raise his hand to answer the question stated: "I think capitalism is what is destroying this country."

Now, please understand that I attended college a little later in life. I was in my early thirties, I was a husband, a father of three, and a combat veteran. I had work, a mortgage, and a lot of responsibilities beyond attending college, so I was not there for the "college experience." I was there to finish my degree. But there was no way I was going to let that student's answer slide without any response. So, I said, "Could you tell me what capitalism is?"

The student began, "Capitalism is a system where an elite hoards resources by exploiting . . ." and I said, "Wait a minute, I'm not really asking for Marx's caricature of capitalism, I'm asking what the actual definition is."

The professor jumped in: "Do you know what it is?"

I said, "Yes, capitalism is an economic system that allows for the private ownership of the means of production, and exchange is voluntary."

The professor looked at me and said, "We can use that." And I'm thinking to myself, well, I certainly hope we can, because that's essentially the definition of a capitalist system.

The other student then looked at me, a little surprised, and I asked him, now that we had a definition, what was his problem with the system I just described? He proceeded to explain that he wasn't a communist or anything, he just thought the truth was somewhere in between.

Well, that is a pretty big concession on his part, going from "it's what's destroying America" to "I'm somewhere in between capitalism and communism." But let's flesh that out a bit.

I said, taking the economic terminology out of it, this is basically a question of two approaches; in capitalism, I own stuff, you own stuff, and the only way we exchange stuff is if we both agree to the exchange. What part of that would you like to exchange for the government owns the stuff and determines for both of us what can be exchanged?

The student, who was very polite by the way, decided he would provide an example of what he was talking about so that I could better understand. He had a friend who was writing a book. In the course of writing this book, it became apparent to his friend that he wasn't going to be able to get it published unless he went through one of these large publishing houses, which "controlled the market." And he would have to pay them to do that, which he considered "unfair."

So, I asked him, what kind of law or regulation was preventing his friend from self-publishing?

His answer was, "Well, no law or anything. It just probably won't be as successful."

So, I responded, "It sounds like your friend wants the benefit of someone else's skills, experience, and resources without paying for them." There was absolutely nothing legal or immoral standing in the way of his friend publishing that book. What his friend wanted was the book deals and book signings and interviews talking about the book, and a company to print out tens of thousands of copies and distribute them in bookstores all over the country . . . but in his mind, that should all just be . . . what? Provided because he was so brilliant?

Nothing is easier than looking at success already achieved and chalking it up to "exploitation." It actually makes us feel better about our own lack of success. The reality is that thousands of people have worked in the publishing business to attain the position they have within the marketplace. Now, I'm certainly not suggesting that every deal has been on the up and up, but on the other side of the equation, in a free market, when you see an opportunity to compete against a company that you feel is failing to meet customer expectations, you have the freedom to do so. Not so in a socialist economy.

So, let's reiterate. Free market capitalism is an economic system that allows for the private ownership of the means of production within a system of voluntary exchange. Implicit in this are a couple of things, not the least of which is respect for property rights, competition, voluntarism, and cooperation.

These attributes of free markets are, I believe, moral in nature. They acknowledge that people have a right to the property they have earned or been given and that to arbitrarily take it away from them constitutes an act of theft. In that sense, I believe that the foundational reason free market capitalism is a superior system is because it is built upon moral concepts.

Of course, the moment you say this, people will point out various excesses or instances of exploitation as evidence of what an absurd belief it is to say that capitalism is moral. But hear me out. I am NOT claiming that everyone who operates in the marketplace is a good guy or behaves in a moral way. I'm saying that respect for property, voluntarism, and individual choice with respect to exchange are moral concepts. People can always choose to exploit a system, no matter how noble you have attempted to make it. Are socialists really claiming that nobody in a position of power has ever exploited the system for their own gain within a socialist or Marxist system? If that were true, they wouldn't have to go around every five minutes explaining how the last attempt at socialism "wasn't real socialism."

Capitalism is morally superior to socialism not because of the people who operate within it but because of how the boundaries and incentive systems within it work with human nature to try and mobilize self-interest toward individual and collective good.

For example, let's say I am a horribly greedy person, and I have an insatiable lust for wealth. Within a capitalist system, I could exploit, lie, and commit fraud in order to attain this wealth, as some have. However, if I get caught engaging in fraud, exploitation, or lying about what my product does, there may be civil or criminal consequences, but there's actually an even more inherent reason why this is not the best approach.

Because capitalism protects voluntary exchange and private property rights, if I lie, cheat, or defraud, I am punished by people refusing to engage in exchange with me. In a capitalist system, customers have the ability to instantly punish a bad producer for whatever reason they see fit, even if formal legal charges are never brought. By contrast, if I focus my efforts on the efficient delivery of goods and services to my customers, they willingly contribute to my goal of being wealthy, not because of my interest, but because I am serving their interests. Capitalism rewards cooperation and the efficient use of resources.

Again, people will often point to waste within a capitalist system and scoff at the idea of "efficiency," but the most important question you should ask is "compared to what?" While it is true that some producers are not very efficient, they are eventually beaten out by producers who are.

You could argue that the world doesn't need dozens of salad dressings in the salad dressing aisle. But if that's true, some of those salad dressings are going to go away as unpopular or unprofitable. But if the government limits the number of salad dressings, there's no reason to think they will be the right ones.

What about the people who have more money than they deserve? Those people exist, but they are always benefiting from government protection from the market. The solution in that case is probably less government, not more.

Let's contrast this with a socialist system, where the government owns the means of production. The idea behind this arrangement is that people "elect" those in power, and they now have power over the state-managed production. Because the state-run plant or factory is owned by "the people," it operates based on what is best for the general public instead of the profit motive. Nice in theory, but what sort of incentive structure is created?

When the state controls the means of production, the "customer" becomes not "the people" but the government officials in charge of the operation. Because competition is not allowed, customers can complain to a bureaucracy, but they cannot choose to shop elsewhere. What we see over time is that state-run enterprises don't like sassy customers. Instead of being aggrieved customers, they become enemies of the state, because after all, they're not publicly criticizing a company like Walmart or Costco, they are attacking "the people's grocery store!" All of a sudden, honest critiques become subversive behavior designed to demoralize the workers and the peace. You can say that is extreme all you like, but how much outspoken criticism of state-run enterprises do you think takes place in China, North Korea, or Cuba?

Most people who say they like socialism actually like a Scandinavian-style safety net, which is high taxes on a high-performing capitalist economy. That's an argument about ideal taxation levels, not the merits of capitalism.

Bottom line, I first defend free markets not on the grounds that they produce better results with respect to the effective and efficient delivery of goods and services but on the basis that they create the proper incentives for human nature.

LESSON 52

HOW TO TEACH YOUR KIDS TO DATE

1. Give them a goal, not just rules.

2. Establish boundaries.

3. Reward good decisions with trust.

4. Be careful what influences you let into your kids' lives, from TV to social media to friends.

Out of all the little nuggets I have thrown out over the years, this is the one that receives the most skepticism and pushback.

I was on the *Iced Coffee Hour* podcast with Graham Stephan and Jack Selby a while back, and the topic of dating and relationships came up. I mentioned that in our house, we didn't let our kids date until they were eighteen, because the purpose of dating was marriage.

Graham and Jack politely pushed back a little and asked if that was wise or even achievable in today's world. They were shocked, and I think a little skeptical, when I told them I hadn't received any real pushback from my son or two daughters. Once it was revealed that we homeschooled, Graham and Jack seemed to think that probably explained it. And it does, but not in the way they assumed.

It's true that our kids were not constantly under pressure five days a week to discuss "who they liked" and "who liked so and so" and "who they were into" by a bunch of other teenagers, none of whom possessed the emotional or intellectual maturity to be engaging in romantic relationships, but it was more than that.

We weren't just giving our kids a set of arbitrary rules to obey. We were setting them up with a completely different mindset regarding relationships, one that was rooted in respect for themselves, their body, their heart, and respect for others. It's fascinating to me that people will endlessly complain about modern dating and then simultaneously reject any approach that doesn't fit into popular trends. I once pointed out that if the current trends worked, there wouldn't be so many people complaining. Maybe we should stop taking dating advice from people with high body counts and twenty-seven exes, all of them "toxic." And yet, when I lay out the guidelines we gave our kids, they are seen as "unrealistic" or "too draconian." But you know what? My oldest daughter is happily married, my son is very respectful toward women and is working to be the kind of man who will attract the kind of woman he wants to marry, and my youngest daughter is confident in herself and not emotionally scarred by a bunch of bad experiences. So, all due respect, but maybe our system is working?

Here are our guidelines.

1. **Get you squared away first.** If your relationship with God is not where it should be, you need to work on that first. This is not just some cutesy cliché. It's real. When you are solid in your relationship with Christ, you know who you are, and you know that you have meaning, value, and

purpose, apart from anyone else. If you start dating when you're a hollow mess, you may attract the kind of person who would only date someone who is a hollow mess.

2. **Dating is not "just for fun." The goal is marriage.** If there's no way you can see yourself married to a person, then don't date them. "But what about giving them a chance? You never know." Yeah . . . you usually do. And if circumstances change where you could see yourself marrying them, then good, you waited instead of starting a romantic relationship before it was ready.

3. **Date for values first.** Looks, interests, goals, ambitions, expectations, communication, and personality can all be incredibly valuable aspects to consider in another human being. But none of those other categories can overcome values and worldview. That's the foundation. If you prize piety, honesty, and generosity, it doesn't matter how much else you have in common with a person who is indifferent to those. If you love America and Marvel movies, it's going to be much easier to live with a person who hates Marvel and loves America than loves Marvel and hates America.

4. **Don't get physical before marriage.** I'm not saying that you can't hug, hold hands, or even respectfully kiss before you get married; I'm simply saying that regardless of what the "How will you know if you're sexually compatible?" crowd says, sex is the easiest thing to figure out between two people in a loving and respectful marriage. If the other person has a high body count, a long list of kinks, a powerful disinterest in having sex, or a porn addiction (or you do!), that's a 1 to 3 problem, not a 4 problem. The reason that avoiding physical activity is so important is that once you indulge, you'll likely ignore a mountain of

red flags to get back into bed. It's why you need to fall in love with and marry the person first. Then you two can enjoy each other physically, and not only will this help you avoid mistakes, but it will also enrich your sex life, because neither one of you has to wonder if you're being compared to someone else or a past experience.

5. **Don't put yourself in compromising situations.** The best way to avoid making mistakes is to not put yourself in positions where they are easily made. I heard one guy word it this way: Avoiding the devil is easier than resisting him.

6. **When you do start dating, be honest with one another.** I'm a big believer that dating and engagements are not supposed to be things that go on for years and years. Unless there is some very good and concrete reason why you are waiting on something, extra-long dating and engagement seasons start to give the impression that you are holding out just in case something better comes along. If through your dating experience you don't feel a burning desire to get married, then the longer you wait, the more opportunity for mistakes, cheating, wasting each other's time, and so on. Just be honest with people so that you can both move on. There will always be a sense of rejection, but that's preferable to delayed rejection, when you already knew what you were going to do. (Not getting physical before marriage tends to fix this problem, as no one wants to wait for years to have sex with someone they're not in love with.)

7. **The rules apply to both sons and daughters.** Nothing is more counterproductive than following one set of rules for your sons and a different set for your daughters. It's true that certain mistakes can affect boys and girls differently, but there are no mistakes that are bad for one but okay

for the other. Good fathers don't allow their sons to become the sort of guys you tell your daughters to avoid.

8. **Model a good relationship for your kids, and they will listen to your advice.** Want your kids to listen to you when it comes to relationships? Then give them a picture of one they want. How Mom and Dad treat each other is setting the example for your kids and will instruct them on whether your advice is worth anything.

Like with all the little tidbits of wisdom and personal experiences I have had, I wish I could have applied all of these as well as I expressed them here. But whether executed to perfection or a lesson learned from a mistake, I believe these guidelines work and have already seen them work for my own children so far.

Don't ever let anyone make you feel guilty for setting boundaries for your children that you didn't have when you were their age. Your job as a parent is not to let them fall into every trap you fell into but to learn from both your successes and your failures to help them navigate a complex and tricky world. It's one thing to let them "figure some things out" or experience a "little pain" when it comes to life's challenges. But it is the relationships with other people in our lives, especially the intimate ones, that have the greatest capacity to leave deep scars. Don't throw your kids into that world in the mistaken belief that they can "figure it out." Guide them, using every tool you have available, so that you can set them up for success in the most important relationship they will ever have with another human being.

LESSON 53

HOW TO TEACH YOUR KIDS TO LOVE AMERICA

1. Your country doesn't have to exist.

2. It exists because people believed that it was worth establishing, other people believed it was worth building, others believed it was worth dying for, and now it is your job to determine if you believe the same things.

3. Strive for better for your country, but understand that it wasn't perfect before, isn't perfect now, and won't be in the future. Guess what, neither is anybody else's country.

4. Saving your country begins with your family.

A nation is not the same thing as a government. We often think of it in those terms, and perhaps for good reason, since politics plays such a large role in the shaping of a nation, from its laws to its ability to defend itself. But a country that derives its entire identity based on its system of government becomes little more than a tax farm for those who control the guys with machine guns.

One of the most unique aspects of the American experiment was the focus on the government's responsibility to the freedom of its citizens, rather than what people owed to the Crown. Another was the notion that governments, especially those governing large areas of diverse peoples, should be strictly limited in scope and power.

We have obviously gotten away from that. But that doesn't absolve us from trying to get it back. And it starts with your family.

If you spend a good part of your day arguing with strangers and none of your day actually explaining, I mean really explaining, why you believe what you do to your children, then you really shouldn't be surprised when you eventually lose the hearts and minds of both the rando online and your children.

Personal responsibility is a hallmark of individual liberty. "Liberty" without responsibility is licentiousness. Licentiousness leads to degeneracy, and degeneracy is the most corrosive element when it comes to preserving a free society. So, before we get into explaining to our children the difference between "democracy" and a constitutional republic, before we explain the problems with inflationary monetary policy, arrogant foreign policy, or tax policy, have we taught our kids personal responsibility?

So, teach your children to take responsibility for their actions and thoughts. Teach them that not every disparity is an "injustice." If you teach them that you should focus more on the things you can control rather than complaining about the things you can't, they will more likely than not become the sort of person who sees opportunities where others see difficulties or "privilege." Your children will have a mindset that directs them toward improving their situation through their own efforts and collaboration with like-minded people; instead of complaining or blaming others, they will most likely be successful.

People who are confident in their abilities and take responsibility for their actions are far less likely to be convinced that what the world needs are more bureaucrats and politicians stealing from people in order to selectively redistribute property in ways that best ensure their reelection rather than addressing any real societal issues.

CLOSING ARGUMENTS

Well, there it is. Just like I promised, neither perfect nor comprehensive, but hopefully useful.

There is a lot more to be said, and maybe there will be another time, but here's what I hope you get from this.

The world needs good men.

I know we are living through what is perhaps the first time in human history where a significant sector of the population is questioning our necessity, but remember, they are able to do that only because of the perseverance of the men who came before us. Those men with all of their flaws created a world so full of creature comforts, so abundant in food and medicine, and so devoid of threats to our safety that people have the ability to arrogantly assume it's their birthright instead of an existence earned through a great deal of toil and sacrifice.

Such is the nature of comfort that when experienced for too long, we forget that it isn't the natural order of things. But here we are.

We find ourselves hurtling toward the "bad times" that "weak men" have created. And many of us want to shout from the rooftops, "Weak men are what you asked for!" And the sad reality is that it is true. Not everyone, mind you, but enough of them. Some of them are still screaming for it even as the consequences of such actions become more apparent. What I'm asking you to do is not listen to them.

They can ask for weak men, demand them, even incentivize them, but what they can't do is compel us to become them. And we can't. I refuse to.

I refuse to for my children.
I refuse to for my wife.
I refuse to for my country.

And if I had none of these things, I would still refuse to because God didn't create me to stand by silently while the barbarians plunder our civilization. He created me to fight for the things I love.

So, I will. This is the hill I die on. And I want those who think they can take my country or fundamentally alter it in ways that betray its very character to know that I will fight them for every inch of ground. I cannot be bribed or threatened. If they want it, come and take it.

And while I can't promise you we will win, I do believe that any mindset not committed to the task at hand will fail.

So, men, let's get to it.

Live your life as if it matters, and never forget that it is far more important to be concerned about what God will say when you arrive than what people will say when you're gone.

Godspeed.

ABOUT THE AUTHOR

NICK FREITAS has been married to his high school sweetheart, Tina, since 1999. Immediately following high school, Nick joined the Army and served with the 82nd Airborne Division and 25th Light Infantry Division as an infantryman. After September 11th, Nick volunteered for US Army Special Forces (Green Berets) and eventually served two tours in Iraq as a Special Forces Weapons Sergeant and Special Forces Intelligence Sergeant. In 2015, he was elected to the Virginia House of Delegates and currently serves on the Finance, Courts of Justice, Public Safety, and Education committees. Nick and Tina have three children and live in Culpeper, Virginia.